THE Mommy BUSINESS

To Lauren

Happy Mothering

& God bless

M. Mate

MICHELE MATHEWS

THE *Mommy* BUSINESS

how to organize and enjoy your family and
still have time to shave your legs!

TATE PUBLISHING
AND ENTERPRISES, LLC

This book is designed to provide accurate and authoritative information with regard to the subject matter covered. This information is given with the understanding that neither the author nor Tate Publishing, LLC is engaged in rendering legal, professional advice. Since the details of your situation are fact dependent, you should additionally seek the services of a competent professional.

The opinions expressed by the author are not necessarily those of Tate Publishing, LLC.

Published by Tate Publishing & Enterprises, LLC
127 E. Trade Center Terrace | Mustang, Oklahoma 73064 USA
1.888.361.9473 | www.tatepublishing.com

Tate Publishing is committed to excellence in the publishing industry. The company reflects the philosophy established by the founders, based on Psalm 68:11,
"The Lord gave the word and great was the company of those who published it."

Book design copyright © 2011 by Tate Publishing, LLC. All rights reserved.
Cover design by Kenna Davis
Interior design by Sarah Kirchen

Published in the United States of America

ISBN: 978-1-61346-931-6
1. Family & Relationships / Parenting / Motherhood
2. Family & Relationships / General
11.10.25

Dedication

This book is dedicated to the Lord, who has blessed me more than any woman deserves to be blessed...

To my husband Frank, who is so patient and supportive. You will always be my light across a crowded room.

To my children and grandchildren, a humongous thank you for allowing me to tell my stories of your childhood... What can I say? You're funny! Thank you for making my job so much fun. I've dreamed of each of you my entire life. No mother could be more proud.

And to my mom and dad for teaching me how to really enjoy my children.

Laughter really is the best medicine.

To Tommy and Cindy. Wish you were here.

Acknowledgements

With extreme gratitude to my writers' group girlfriends, Robyn, Cindy and Cheryl, who tirelessly encouraged me to write this book.

Table of Contents

Quotes to Live By

Laughter is the best medicine.

Erma Bombeck

Chaos in the midst of chaos isn't funny, but chaos in the midst of order is…

Steve Martin

Your antique, expensive and irreplaceable watch being flushed down the commode by your two year old is just a moment in time meant to make you laugh later… right?

Michele E. Mathews

Introduction

Frank and I have been happily married for twenty years, two months, and six days... but who's counting? Once I said "I do", I instantly became a stepmother to Kellie, who was nine years old at the time. Soon after, the boys came and came and came! Three babies in three years! At one point Chris, Josh, and Sean were all in diapers and still taking bottles. We called them our baby assembly line.

During this challenging time with three babies at home with no money for Mother's Day Out programs and Kellie beginning the tween-whatever years, we moved eight times in nine years. Frank was moving up the ladder with his job, which was a financial blessing but truly a time-commitment hardship on our family life.

I was exhausted, overwhelmed, homesick, and, to make matters worse, I never saw my husband due to his work schedule. By the end of each day, we were each too tired to even say goodnight.

It is in the face of extreme difficulty that most people rise to the occasion and muster the determination to turn an otherwise unworkable situation into something wonderful. This was certainly the choice I was faced with.

Today, Chris is nineteen years old, Josh is eighteen, and Sean is fifteen and two-thirds years old. (Anything to get closer to that magical age of sixteen to be able to drive the family truck.) Kellie is thirty-one years old, married, and the mother to our two grandchildren, Melanie and Jacob, ages eight and ten.

Frank and I are very proud of our children. We are frequently complimented on their good manners, respectfulness, and dedication to having successful lives of their own. They have been selected good citizens, they participate in National Honor Society, and they excel in music, sports, and their college courses. They are each equipped with a healthy sense of humor, and, when together, our home is continuously filled with laughter.

While raising my children, our home was never quiet. The dishwasher and washing machine were on around the clock, the telephone never stopped ringing, and we always seemed to be rushing off to somewhere.

Because of our busy schedules, time is very precious to my family. If only there were fifty hours in a day, we just might have time to fit it all in and not have to rush!

But since we can't change the number of hours in a day, we must instead concentrate on how to make our lives easier, less chaotic, and more productive. Our jobs as mothers, the mommy business, if you will, are like any other business actually. In order to be successful, we must be organized, resourceful, calm, happy within, rested, able to think quickly on your feet, creative, good at financial planning, disciplined, and able to get along well with others.

Mothers are essentially the CEOs of their households.

As with any business, it is important to stay focused. The downfall of the CEO can be the demise of the entire company as well. Upper management, AKA *parents,* must be stable and in control; otherwise the trickle-down effect can be catastrophic.

All families are on the run these days; however, there are certain fundamentals of raising children that cannot go by the wayside without serious consequences. In our world today, most families are suffering from sleep deprivation, chaos, disorganization, and lack of discipline.

Because of these issues, there are a lot of families that are unable to find the time or energy to truly enjoy being together. Your family doesn't have to fall into this category.

By changing a few simple things within your family— such as sleep routines, family responsibilities, discipline techniques, and time management—most mothers will find they have the energy to concentrate on being more creative, patient, and loving not only to their husbands and children but to themselves as well.

When you read this book, I do not want to give any false illusions such as "we eat dinner every night together come rain or shine," or "my boys never fight with each other," or "Frank and I idolize each other every second of every day."

Trust me. This is not the case. My boys *do* fight, we do *not* eat together as a family every night, and sometimes Frank is so *completely unreasonable* that I have to find it in my heart to forgive him time and time again... (He is always wrong. It's weird!)

With baseball practice, dance lessons, laundry, etc., it's unreasonable to think that we are going to accomplish any of these ideologies 100 percent of the time. (If you are in this percentage range, *you* need to write a book!) However, I do want moms to have ideas and goals to strive for so that there will be more time and love left over to pass around within their families.

I have written his book for you ladies so that you can find your purpose again. This book contains fresh ideas for you to experiment with so that you can be the mother you always dreamed of being… the one that wasn't so tired and overwhelmed. I want to nurse your spirit with laughter, and I want you to fall in love with your husband all over again.

There is no other creature on earth that is more beautiful, more loving, nurturing, more alive than a mother. Whether you are a working mother or an at-home mother, you are the CEO of your own mommy business. There is no other human on this planet that is more qualified for the job of taking care of your family than you. I am going to help you make your home life a success so that everyone you love can not only thrive within but have a great time as well!

So sit back, relax, and enjoy the journey through *The Mommy Business.*

Bringing Home the Bacon vs. Making the Bacon: Working Moms and At-Home Moms

Today is the big day at school. On Family Day at Taylor Elementary, the children get to tell all about each member of their family. The teachers will be asking a lot of questions like, How many brothers and sisters do you have? Where does your daddy work? and Does your mommy work or stay at home?"

Seven-year-old Ben is ready. When the teacher asks, "Who would like to share their family story first?" his hand shoots up sky high.

"Okay, Ben, let's hear about your family first. Come up to the front of the class, please."

Ben rushes to the front of the classroom and stands by Mrs. Blackburn's desk. "My family is the best family in the universe," Ben begins. "There are four people in our family. I have one little brother, Charlie. He's only four years old. He bugs me most of the time, but sometimes he's okay."

Mrs. Blackburn smiles and asks, "Ben, tell us what kind of work your father does."

"Oh, that's easy, my dad brings home the bacon!" Ben says enthusiastically.

"Brings home the bacon?" Mrs. Blackburn asks, dumbfounded.

"Yes, my mom is always telling my dad, 'Honey, let's get this straight. You may bring home the bacon, but I *make* the bacon!'" Ben concludes proudly, "That's what my mom and dad do for work. My dad brings home the bacon, and my mom makes it!"

Ben could care less who comes home with the actual check. He is proud of the work his parents do regardless of their titles because this family dynamic works to create a happy, daily routine in his world. That said, if either of his parents falls down on the job, his family life will no doubt suffer.

Whew. There are certain conversations people should avoid at all costs when in the presence of mothers:

- For at-home-moms, staying home isn't considered real work.

- For working moms, working outside the home is considered abandoning her children.

Man, oh, man, nothing sets off a mom who stays at home to care for her family more than a belittling validation of her profession.

She may not earn a paycheck, but her bacon-makin' services are beyond compensation. Mothers are without a doubt the backbone of every family. At-home mothers are at it twenty-four seven. No lunch breaks, no salary adjustments for a job well done, no time away on the weekends, and no vacation.

On the opposite side of the spectrum, working moms are bringing home the bacon, makin' the bacon, and doing everything else in between!

Like the stay at-home-moms, their choice of working outside the home is sometimes challenging as well. Society attacks our working mothers for not staying home to raise their children; they place undeserved guilt on mothers who work, as though they are abandoning their children in place of a career.

For some women, their careers may be something they've worked all their lives to attain. They've worked hard to maintain good family foundations alongside of their working goals. Women are capable of anything. With the proper balance, it is possible to provide a loving and supportive home for your children and balance a career too.

There are a lot of working mothers that would love to stay home and raise their families, but financially it just isn't possible, just as there are many stay-at-home moms that would love to be back in the hustle and bustle of work again but would feel guilty leaving their families.

A mother's life can be such an emotional tug of war. We are simultaneously pulled in so many different directions that sometimes it is hard to keep track of which end is up.

One thing is for sure: whether a working mother or an at-home mother, we love our children. There will always be pros and cons to each scenario.

THE GRASS IS ALWAYS GREENER ON THE OTHER SIDE

From the Perspective of the At-Home Mother
Stay-at-home mothers appreciate the fact that staying home to raise the children is a luxury and is deeply appreciated. They love experiencing the first smile, first steps, even nursing a sick child back to health.

At-home moms take pride in their children's accomplishments and are involved with their schools, know the good teachers to request, and are homeroom mothers. The children love their moms to volunteer at school.

At-home moms are team moms for sports and snack moms for dance recitals. They teach their toddlers nursery rhymes and ABCs over peanut butter and jelly sandwiches. Picnics in the park are a once-a-week planned event. They are involved with mothers groups at church, and they teach Sunday school.

Their houses are usually tidy, and they are conscientious about having a well-balanced meal on the table for dinner. A lot of at-home moms exercise to stay in shape as well.

But as with most of us from time to time, the grass is greener on the other side. There are some days at-home moms miss having an intelligent conversation. The story of Peter Rabbit for the one-hundredth time just doesn't quite cut the mustard.

They find themselves reciting multiplication facts while driving in the car. Some days, these moms swear that if they hear, "See the birdie?" one more time from the back seat, they are going to completely implode.

Their husbands come home and mistakenly tell their wives about their lunch at the Palm Restaurant downtown and how wonderful their filet tasted, forgetting she had cheerios and a leftover banana. Big mistake.

Like it or not, at-home moms miss the outside world from time to time. Sometimes they feel cut off from anything grown up.

These moms have traded their high heels and skirts for tennis shoes and sweat pants. Wearing lipstick is saved for church, and they can't remember the last time someone asked for their opinion. They wonder if they even have an opinion anymore that doesn't pertain to car seats and how to treat spit-up stains.

Even though they feel blessed to stay at home with their precious children, most at-home moms feel, at some point, envious of mothers who have a career. Some days at-home mothers wonder if they made the right choice.

The Palm Restaurant sounds great, but an at-home mom would settle for an uninterrupted hamburger any day of the week.

From the Perspective of the Working Mother:
The working mother goes to work every day and has developed several close relationships with the girls in her office. They have gift exchanges at Christmas, birthday lunches, and shop together at lunchtime.

She takes pride in her professional appearance and has a standing appointment every other Friday to have her nails done.

Her home is usually a little tidier than the at-home moms' homes because the children attend school or stay at a daycare while she is working. Some are even able to employ a cleaning service as well.

Just last week she got a promotion for helping her boss on a project that they had been working on for six months. To celebrate, her coworkers took her out to dinner. The jubilation she felt was indescribable.

The working mother loves her children and keeps up with their schoolwork and basketball games on the weekend. She cooks dinner a few times a week and reads to the children before bedtime. She prides herself on kissing the children good-bye in the morning and tucking each one in bed at night.

She stays up until midnight most nights, wrapping Christmas gifts, making Halloween costumes, finishing the children's photo albums, folding clothes, and paying bills.

The working mother learned long ago to operate on only a few hours of sleep each night.

For most working mothers, the schedule runs her down, and she is exhausted from living two such demanding lives. Sometimes she would love to trade places with an at-home mother, but providing a solid college fund for her children is more important to her. She refuses to quit work because if she does, Tommy doesn't get piano lessons, Jessica can forget about braces, and little Andrew would have to do without new roller blades.

Without her income, there would be no Disneyland, no new bicycle for Christmas, and no prom dresses. She works to provide the family with the extras they wouldn't be able to afford with only one income. And though tired, she continues on because it's the only way she can give her family all the opportunities she otherwise could not afford.

She doesn't allow herself to think about missing her children's school parties and her baby's first steps. Instead she gears up to make up on the weekends for lost time during the week.

Superwoman doesn't have a thing on the working mom. The working mom is super human. She truly does it all. And the Palm Restaurant for lunch? Given the choice, she'd rather have cheerios and bananas with her children any day.

BLOOM WHERE YOU'RE PLANTED

Whether you are a stay-at-home mom or a working mom, try your best to bloom where you're planted. By this I mean make the most of whatever situation you are in.

When my husband came home with the news from his company that we were being transferred to California (the first of eight transfers), I was devastated. We had just moved into our dream home, and we had friends I couldn't fathom leaving behind. I had always been one to rebound, but leaving our home, friends, and family seemed an insurmountable emotional feat.

We sat on the floor of our living room after we put the children to bed that night and talked until the wee hours of the morning, weighing each option carefully as to what was the best thing to do for our family. He was moving up the ladder of his company, and to say no to an opportunity could be professional suicide. That night, my husband and I made a pact. We decided that as long as we were all together, any four walls would be considered *home,* and any city we lived in would be considered an adventure. That very night, my husband and I made the decision to make the most of wherever we landed, to "*bloom where we were planted.*" Because of our openness to enjoy our lives as they unfolded, we have memories to cherish and even more friends that will live in our hearts forever.

Acceptance is a beautiful thing. When we stop wasting our precious energy yearning for lives other than our own, something wonderful happens: we learn to love the lives we have. So whether you are a working mom or a stay-at-home mom, learn to love the life you have. In this book, we will discuss ways to enhance your life, your health, your happiness, and your marriage. But it all starts with one corny little phrase of complete acceptance:

Bloom where you're planted.

There will always be days you will want to live the life of another, but stay your course of commitment. Both ways of raising a family are valid. The important thing to remember is that you are loved by your family.

A child's love for his mother is unbiased, unconditional, and totally blind. They look up to us whether we look like Victoria's Secret models, cook like Martha Stewart, or have the intelligence of Einstein. Children only care about our love and our time.

I, for one, like being an at-home mom. Though I am envious of my working friends who are getting to dress up every day and have lunch with their work buddies, I have convinced myself that they envy me as well because I haven't shaved my legs in two months.

With so many roles to play, sometimes we mothers find we aren't enjoying our families quite like we should be. Part of this stems from sheer exhaustion, part from chaos, and part from no time to fill your own personal well.

But let's start at the tip of the iceberg: sleep deprivation. Lack of sleep and running on empty may be the culprit to any mother not getting the most out of her life. But before a mom can sleep, the children must be sleeping. So let's dive into the wonder of slumber ...

Climb aboard the Sleepy-Time Train! Your Sleeping Baby

After experiencing complete sleep deprivation, I now recognize a good night's sleep for the precious gift that it is. I am a sane woman with it (I have references) and a crazy one without it.

Top Five Ways To Know You Are Wiped Out

1. By nine p.m. your children are no longer adorable. They become small, loud people with runny noses.

2. You fall asleep unexpectedly on the couch and awake to the children finger painting the walls with jelly.

3. You have a habit of clearing a pathway from your child's bed to yours just so that there are no obstacles in the way while you sprint to bed after kissing them goodnight.

4. You walk by a makeup counter at the mall, just browsing, and the consultant tells you that you

would be perfect for their new, industrial-strength eye concealer.

5.   The idea of having sex with your husband at the end of the day is the funniest thing you've heard in a long time.

One day when my boys were still in diapers, I was thinking to myself how wonderful it would be if I could somehow get both babies to sleep that afternoon … at the same time. Glorious. I sat on my back porch and watched my one- and two-year-old boys romping in the grass outside. They were precious. Healthy and full of energy. So why wasn't I enjoying them more?

As I watched them play, I noticed that my one-year-old, Joshie, had ventured over to the flowerbeds. *I'd better redirect him,* I thought to myself since he had a tendency to eat everything, including my flowers.

By the time I reached him, he had something in his mouth all right; only it wasn't a flower! It was dark in color. At first I panicked because I thought it was a bug! But as I got closer, I realized it was much, much worse. My baby had a mouthful of cat poop! Apparently it looked an awful lot like the link sausage we had for breakfast!

I brought both boys in the house and scrubbed them in the tub until they were beet-red. Unfortunately Christopher had also wondered why the "breakfast sausage" was in the backyard and joyfully covered himself in it as well.

As both babies sat in the tub, wailing in indignation, I too was crying. I dried off my sniffling boys and kept thinking to myself, *I could handle the chaos of motherhood if*

I could just get a little sleep. I hadn't slept through the night in, well… forever. I had to take control. It was sink or swim time for the Mathews family.

At one point in our family lives, all three boys were in diapers and bottles at the same time. Through the sheer desire to survive, my husband and I developed a workable cycle of teamwork and had human assembly lines going night and day. Chances were really high that one of them would get a bottle they didn't want, a nap they didn't need, or a diaper change that wasn't necessary. But it was the only way to cope with three babies under three.

I ultimately made the executive decision that I had to become more organized. First order of business was to put the children on a sleep schedule. In doing this, I was able to accomplish much more during the day without being completely exhausted myself.

Running on empty is no way to raise children. It's no way for Mom and Dad to live either. Children are to be enjoyed and cherished, not endured. However, *no one* is happy when they are overtired. Therefore the first step to a happy family is for everyone involved to have enough rest.

There are several ways to get your children on a sleep schedule. These are a few tips that helped to get my children on the sleepy-time train!

LEARN YOUR BABY'S CRY FOR COMMUNICATION

It's hard to let our babies cry themselves to sleep. There isn't a parent out there who doesn't shiver at the sound of a baby crying. Sometimes mommies and daddies equate a baby's cry with pain. It's simply not true. A baby cries as a means of communication as well as to express uncomfortable situations. Eventually she is able to even learn manipulation by crying. (I know this because I still practice this skill myself from time to time.)

At a very early age, your baby has learned that by crying, he is able to summon you. There is nothing more comforting to your baby than the sound of your voice or the sight of your face. They learn quickly how to get your attention.

So train yourself to recognize your baby's cry. If you listen carefully, they are different. There is a cry of distress, hunger, boredom, pain, and a cry for being uncomfortable, such as with a wet diaper or being cold.

By learning more about your baby and her communication, you are better able to understand her when you begin to put her sleep patterns in place and allow her to cry herself to sleep.

START EARLY AND FOLLOW THROUGH

By the age of six months, your healthy baby is able to sleep through the night without any additional feedings. This is the perfect time to teach him how to soothe himself back to sleep.

I know of several mothers who waited until the child was two years old and older. By this age sleep patterns are not only established, but they are ingrained into the child as routine. If you have been getting up three times a night with Stacy for three years, you are going to have a tough time breaking her of the habit of seeing her mommy in the middle of the night. It's never too late to establish healthy sleep patterns; just keep in mind the older the child, the more difficult it may be.

It's important to ask yourself the following questions before allowing your baby to cry herself to sleep:

1. Is my child healthy?

   Make sure your child has a healthy checkup with your pediatrician before allowing your baby to cry himself to sleep. You want to make sure that he is not crying due to an ear infection you didn't know he had.

2. Is my household stable at this time?

   This question is important to ask yourself because you don't want to start on this new sleep pattern to help your child sleep through the night when you are moving into a new house, expecting company, or planning a vacation. Try to carve out this time to be patient, stress free, and undistracted with other issues.

3. Am I serious about not going back once I've started?

   It's important to make your mind up to follow through with your plan. By letting him cry for an hour and then deciding, "I can't take it anymore!" you are setting yourself up for an even worse night the following night. In this case, you've just taught Johnny that if he holds out, you'll pick him up.

4. Do I have a sleep routine in place?

   You don't want to put any undue distress on your baby by starting cold turkey. Start several weeks in advance by establishing your baby's daily routines such as bath times, meal times, and bed times. Once a schedule is in place, you will be more successful because she will be ready for bed when you begin your new sleep patterns.

According to Dr. Judith Owens, a pediatrician at Brown University, most researchers agree on the following length-of-sleep-per-day estimates based on age:

One year old: 14 hours, including one or two naps

Two years old: 11–12 hours at night, including a single nap during lunchtime that lasts one to two hours

Three years old: 12–12 1/2 total with some kids stopping naps

Four years old: 111/2–12 total hours with less naps

Five years old: 11hours with no naps

Six years old: 10 3/4–11hours

Seven years old: 10 1/2–11hours

Eight years old: 10 1/4–10 3/4 hours

Nine year old: 10–10 1/3 hours

Ten through puberty: 9 3/4 -10 hours.

Teens: 9 1/4 hours

It may seem like forever, but eventually your baby *will* fall off to sleep. Each night will become more routine for him to be in his bed alone. This is a wonderful gift of independence. He will discover that he does not need to be with you every minute in order to feel secure. This is the first step toward his independence and self-confidence ... and yours.

It is ironic that as much as we love our children from the moment we lay eyes on them and feel the intense desire to protect them and hold them to us, our main objective as parents is to make them independent of us. We teach them to hold their bottles on their own, feed themselves solid food, use the potty on their own, and so on.

So it follows that it is also our job to teach them to sleep independently. They need their sleep. Moms and dads need sleep. It's important to make resting a priority in all families. However, while waiting for this transition to take hold, put the jelly on a high shelf and wear lots of eye concealer.

ESTABLISH CALMING ROUTINES FOR INFANTS

Most children respond well to routines starting from the day they come home from the hospital as newborns. Their schedules of night and day may be mixed up, but their behavior almost indicates that they appreciate being corrected and connected to the mainstream.

1. Manipulate a day-time sleep schedule for your baby.
   You may have to tickle some feet and even wake the baby from sleeping too late in the morning, but establish the naptime for your baby with the goal of an early bedtime. If you have an infant that is still taking two naps a day, try to get naps to

take place from nine to eleven a.m. with an after-noon nap from three to five p.m. In this way your baby will be stimulated enough and ready for an 8-p.m. bedtime. Allowing a baby to sleep too long during the day confuses the daytime and night-time hours. Wake your baby if necessary to get on track.

2. Bath time is an extremely important part of the winding-down transition of the day for a baby.
    It becomes a signal that it is time for a long win-ter's nap. This is a cozy, soft, sweet-smelling time of day that will help to signal your child that the quiet part of the day is about to begin. Bath time should also be a scheduled part of the day. With time you may even notice that your baby becomes fussy at his normal bath time because his little body knows that it's time take a warm bath and settle down.

3. Putting your baby to bed at a designated time every night can make all the difference when you allow them to cry themselves to sleep.
    A ritual is a must and you will find that with time you may not need a clock to tell you when it's bed-time because your baby will let you know. Unless of course you're watching the clock already.

Magic Tricks to Get Your Routine in Place

1. Rockin' my baby

   Some moms and dads enjoy rocking their babies to sleep. It is the sweetest part of the day and, I admit, a time I could not resist. However, when you begin your sleeping pattern for your baby, I suggest rocking your baby until he's *almost* asleep. In this way, she and you are not robbed of this special time, yet she is still allowed to fall asleep on her own.

2. Lullaby music

   One of the things I did when our first baby arrived was purchase a child's music carousel. These are available in most discount super centers or department stores and come in various forms. Some attach to the crib, and some carousels sit on their dressers. Some light up, displaying shapes and characters on the ceiling, then turn themselves off in twenty minutes.

3. Music has a calming effect on most babies. As the children grow up, you can buy the storybooks on cassette tapes to drift off to. My boys loved this.

   I began using the music when they were infants and needed their midnight feedings. When I nursed them in the darkness of their rooms, I turned their music boxes on.

   This quickly grew into an association between their mommy's love and warmth and the music that was playing. This association is quite valuable later on when you are no longer feeding them during the night and need them to put themselves back to sleep.

By quietly walking into their rooms and turning on the music box, they no longer needed me. The association was made. In this way I was able to accomplish two goals: I gave the boys the ability to put themselves back to sleep and a positive attitude about going to sleep as well.

Be Prepared for Changing Schedules as Your Children Grow.

As your child grows from an infant into a toddler and so on, his sleep patterns will change greatly. After the age of twelve months, most babies can be manipulated to a once-a-day nap routine. This new schedule will prepare them for an earlier bedtime and a longer sleep schedule throughout the night.

There are, however, other changes that interfere with their sleeping, such as nightmares, illness, and separation anxiety, to name a few. These should not be total interruptions of your child's sleep routines and will eventually subside.

Try to resist the temptation during these periods of change to bring your child into your bed. You may send the wrong signal to your child such as "this is a problem you cannot handle on your own."

It's heartbreaking to have a child with nightmares, but you can help him to overcome these events so much more easily if you reassure him and help him back into his own bed. With the support of their mommies and daddies, most children can conquer these fears and issues. If bedtime behaviors continue or worsen, see your doctor.

Stand Your Ground

In order to get the sleep schedules to work, you must be very determined with your children. In our house, bedtime is bedtime, and there is no negotiating.

If you are confident in yourself and have the best interest of your family in mind, the children will adjust so much easier than if you are wishy-washy and apologetic about your decision making. It becomes a way of life. Mommy and Daddy know what is best, and everyone is happier when their surroundings are non-chaotic and controlled when patterns are being set into place. Stand your ground!

Once you have the sleep routines in place, you are ready for scheduling in other areas of your family.

I cannot express enough how much routines have helped our children as they have grown. They may grow out of naps, but healthy sleep patterns in their own beds are significant when they begin school as well.

Allow for Some Winding-down Time before Lights Out

One of the routines we established when my boys were between the ages of one and two years old was that for thirty minutes before lights out, the boys could look at books in their beds. This is a wonderful way of winding the children down from playtime. It also occupies them while waiting for Mommy or Daddy to read during alone time with each child. This gives a love for books that is beyond measure.

To tell the children it is time to go to bed gets an entirely different reaction from asking them, "Which stories are you going to read tonight?"

I began this bedtime strategy when my boys were still in the crib. Of course, they progressed rapidly from angelic little bunny stories to wizards and sorcery in the dark unknown, but as a mother, I adjusted just fine.

Establish Fun Routines for Your Children!

In addition to reading, you can make going to bed fun for your tots! I have this silly little song and dance routine that I would do sometimes for the boys when I tucked them in bed. I would say it's a cross between really bad ballet and an even worse cheerleading number!

My boys loved to see me look so foolish! What the heck—anything to hear that belly laugh… There's nothing more heartwarming than the sound of a child convulsed in giggles. Be creative! (Disclaimer: Don't try this at home without the consent from your doctor!)

Bedtime should be a snuggly time. I sometimes called myself the cozy patrol, and everyone must be cozy and tucked in properly before going off to Dreamland. (Note: you know you are overdoing it when your husband expects this too.) My children loved Dreamland. We all knew Dreamland was fantasy, yet we discussed what's going on there each night. It was always directly related to what they are interested in. (Again, if your husband asks, "What's going on in Dreamland today?" your family has crossed the line from reality completely.)

For Sean, Dreamland might have had puppet shows and a playground made of candy so that after you slide, you can eat it when you're finished.

On the sleepy-time train that carries you to Dreamland, they are always serving an imaginary snack. One day it's hot chocolate with whipped cream, Christopher's favorite. Another day it's chocolate-chip ice cream for Josh. You just never know what to expect in Dreamland. The sky's the limit, and every night it changes.

A journey to Dreamland fills children's imaginations and gives some grand ideas to fall asleep with rather than a simple goodnight and a closing of the door.

This type of imagination can be especially helpful when children begin having bedtime fears. It plants fun, colorful thoughts into their minds to dwell on instead of their fear.

Special Blankies or Animals

Some children need their special blankets or animals to feel secure while sleeping. There is nothing wrong with this. In fact, I encourage lovies. It is an expression of love and nurturing behavior for both girls and boys.

Whatever makes your child feel warm, cozy, secure, and have a good attitude about bedtime, do it. Sleeping is a natural part of our lives. The longer parents put off teaching good habits, the more traumatizing it will be for the children in the long run. So start early.

Get on board the sleepy-time train with your children, and join us in Dreamland!

ONCE YOU'VE GOTTEN THE CHILDREN TO BED, DEVOTE THE EVENING TO YOURSELVES! (YOU AND YOUR HUSBAND)

Once you've gotten all of your little ones on a schedule of sleeping through the night and going to bed at an earlier time, you have the time to devote to yourselves as a couple.

Parents love their children. But all couples need peace and quiet at some point during the day. Remember, you are a couple first, last, and in between.

I'm not suggesting that enough sleep for your family will solve all your problems or keep your children from eating kitty sausage in your backyard. But you will have a lot more energy to scrub them down with the proper rest. You might even find your sense of humor again and chuckle.

Organizing Your Crib: Taking Control of Your Home and Time

The alarm goes off. It's seven a.m., and I'm making coffee before I'm even aware that I'm standing in my kitchen. It was all part of our morning routine to get the boys off to kindergarten and elementary school.

- Make coffee.

- Wake boys.

- Start breakfast.

- Listen to the boys say they don't want breakfast.

- Force them to at least drink their juice and take one bite so that they have the energy to feed the dog.

- Remind them to make their beds, brush the velvet buildup off their teeth, and comb hair while I make lunches.

- Go over spelling words and hand out school picture money.

- Try to make sure Sean is wearing underwear to school by reminding him that he can hurt his penis if he zips it up in his jeans after urinating.

- Hang my head in despair when I've failed to get the message across as he tells me bluntly, "Big boys don't have to wear underwear."

I sip my coffee while secretly praying that the teacher doesn't go with him to the bathroom. I recite quietly to myself, "Pick your battles, pick your battles." I guess wearing underwear should not be a huge issue... not as big as flushing the toilet *once in a while*.

I make a note to myself to make flushing a new priority for the boys. Once everyone is dressed and ready, I kiss them all good-bye as they board the school bus, and I begin my day. Whew. My day. I so mistakenly thought that when I got all the children off to school that I would have this luxurious day all to myself. I would watch Oprah, Regis and Kathy Lee, and eat Cheetos by the bagful. Well, unfortunately, the only thing that has materialized is the way I've found time to eat Cheetos.

I am no natural Cinderella, so by the time I complete the daily transformation, I'm off to make my homeroom kindergarten meeting at nine thirty a.m. for the Valentine's Day party, work an hour in the work center cutting out dye-cuts for the bulletin board, then quickly slam the peanut butter and jelly sandwich that I've packed.

After I leave school, it's time to deposit Frank's check, drop by the cleaners, pick up Christopher's new prescription glasses, swing by the drugstore to pick up Josh's inhaler, buy milk, and get home in time for the repairman to come to repair my broken freezer before I lose everything in it.

While he's fixing the freezer, I begin sautéing my stew meat for dinner, and in between stirring it, I am paying bills and scheduling appointments for the eye doctor. The phone never stops ringing from four p.m. on at my house because every solicitor in the country has figured out that I'm home, waiting for the boys to get off the bus.

I know our days may vary in the errands we run and duties we have as mothers, depending on the ages of our children. However, most mommies reading this book probably have days that closely resemble mine in some form or fashion. Moms are busy!

Being organized is the only thing that a mom can truly count on in the mommy business. We can plan on an appointment that we've made, but appointments can cancel. We can look forward to finally having lunch with a girlfriend, but our youngest will most certainly come down with a fever that day.

Mommies can have the best of all intentions, but if their lives are unorganized, family life can become complicated.

My methods for being organized are neither costly nor highly technical. I do not need a computerized database in my purse but rather a small notebook and a large calendar. Simplicity at its best, and it works like a charm.

HAZEL

My most trusted pal is a little notepad I call "Hazel." Remember Hazel? The loveable family housekeeper that was always getting herself out of trouble from the TV show back in the 70s? Perhaps I am dating myself here, but I loved that show. Hazel always made everyone around her look good.

This method of being organized is not sophisticated, hard to maintain, or high maintenance. Hazel is not made of fancy materials. She is instead a yellow five-by-seven pad of paper that comes five to a pack at the drug store for a dollar and ninety-nine cents.

Hazel has a list of everything I need to do that day, what I didn't get done yesterday, and the phone numbers I jotted down in the car last Wednesday.

She carries the dinner plans that I made with the PTA president, reminders to change the oil in the car, a note on my foolish commitment to bake four cakes for the Fall Festival, and the final notice to wire money to the electric company *today!*

A notebook like this is an absolute lifesaver for all moms. My purse selection is no longer made by style or type of leather but most definitely on where and how Hazel and my cell phone will fit comfortably. I am way past fashion.

Each morning while my coffee is brewing, I get Hazel out. I look at yesterday's list and add my leftover to dos to today's list. It's the little things that we forget in our daily routines that make for a stressful existence. Like … forgetting Bunko is at your house tomorrow night, forgetting baseball tryouts, or forgetting your OB appointment that took you six months to book.

If moms can get used to putting everything into their notebooks routinely, the small things get done. This gives way to a less stressed out mom because she is not constantly overwhelmed by her life.

THE CAPTAIN

While my Hazel is small and unassuming, the "captain" is large and in charge! Captain Kangaroo was the man. He had the best ideas and always had control. The captain calendar hangs on our bulletin board in the kitchen, easily accessible to the entire family. A permanent figure, visible, reliable, and full of information, he is available at all times.

Every night, *before* each new day, I take a glance to make sure that I have that fresh apple for Christopher's apple science experiment or that I paid the five dollars to the lady at the PTA who has called me three times this week. (This, of course, is not an exact science.)

The secret to the calendar is to write things down the moment you're committing to them, if possible. If you're making a doctor's appointment, write it down. If you're signing up to bring cookies for the Christmas cookie swap down the street, write it down. Then write it down on the day before so you will remember to *make* them.

Like Hazel, I cannot function without my captain. It helps jog your memory for anniversaries, the company picnic, and pajama day at school. You can forget a lot of things, but if you forget pajama day and Tiffany was the only one without pajamas and her special bear, you may be in some hot water that night.

I have learned over the years that by keeping careful track of such events, we have cut down on the crises in our lives. Children can be so devastated by missing out on extra-curricular activities, and, frankly, as much as my boys love me, the excuse "honey, I forgot" has never sufficiently healed their hysteria.

Try to purchase your calendar as soon as the New Year's ones are available. You can acquire your very own captain at any local office-supply store. But by doing so early, you are able to write in school events for the year, such as early dismissals, teacher birthdays, winter parties, your husband's company picnic, and what day of the month to give your dog his heartworm medicine.

I can even arrange for babysitters when I see that by the miracle of miracles, the boys don't have a baseball game or other social obligation, and Frank and I can go out to dinner with friends on a real, live date!

PRIORITIZE YOUR DAY

As mothers we can never predict our days. We've said before mommies may plan for it to go one way, but there is always the possibility for enormous change. By being organized, mommies are able to roll with the punches and make the most of the hand we're dealt.

One of the reasons for writing down your list of things to do is so that they are concrete until taken care of and crossed off. Try to plan to accomplish a few of your priorities on your list each day.

You may have a child home from school with fever. Originally you planned to take care of some banking, return the singing topiary you received as an anniversary gift, and buy some new socks for your husband. Not today. Instead go back through your Hazel and find what you can accomplish at home. Maybe it's cleaning out that cabinet under the kitchen sink or venturing into your refrigerator vegetable drawer to play the game *guess what the goo in the baggie used to be*. During naptime and in between caring for your sick little one, try to accomplish something while they rest.

There is something to be said about accomplishment and its direct link with our sense of pride in our work. The mommy business is no different than any other job really. There is a joy in getting things done, being in charge of your job. Being a successful mommy always begins with being organized.

Happy Scenario:

Organization=Self Esteem = Personal
Happiness = Family Happiness

At the end of every day, you should feel good about what you've been able to achieve in addition to all the hugs you give and the boo boos you kiss and make better.

We have started with the most basic necessities of the at-home mom. The sooner you get your family scheduled, ultimately, the happier you all will be.

With a properly rested family and an organized household, what else could you possibly wish for other than for your children to be successfully potty trained? Let's continue on for some fun ideas to get your child excited about using the potty and some realistic reasons why you should slow down and let them run this show!

Diapers Forever? Ideas for the Potty-training Mommy

"So, Jane, is Sarah ever going to get out of those diapers? She is two years old, for goodness' sake!" her sister-in-law Angela chides snidely. "You know, Anna was trained by the time she was a year and a half! You'd better get on the ball, or Sarah will be going to her first prom in Pull-Ups!" she snickers.

The pressure is on. Jane flashes forward to Sarah, sixteen years old, getting ready for her prom. Beautiful dress, up-do hair, corsage, painted fingernails... and Pull-Ups. Horrified, she shakes the image out of her mind. Determined to start potty training Sarah in the morning, she stops by the store and purchases big-girl panties on the way home.

To make herself feel better about her sister-in-law's comments, Jane reminds herself that Angela has a bald spot on the back of her head. She laughs villainously all the way home. Lesson to be learned here: Don't ever criticize a potty-training mother.

I too was a victim of this myth. I too began to feel that when my first child turned two years old, he should innately want to use the toilet. I mean, aren't *all* children ready to be potty trained by their second birthdays? And if not, what was *I* doing wrong as a mommy?

Most experts say that children are ready to *begin* the toilet-training process at approximately eighteen to twenty-four months. This opinion varies of course.

"The control of the sphincter muscle does not become voluntary until the age of eighteen months," according to Vicki Lansky, author of *Vicki Lansky's Practical Parenting, Toilet Training.* Therefore, we can hardly expect children to control their bodily functions at this age when they are in the primary stages of this development. Needless to say, there are exceptions to any rule.

A child that is potty trained early does not make the parent an exceptional parent, nor should the parent of a late bloomer feel like a loser. The child's ability to be toilet trained in no way is a reflection of the parents' proficiency. Success or failure, it seems, is mostly dependent upon the child's own personal timing, not ours. Rushing a child to use the potty before they are ready would be like rushing me through the exit of the annual shoe sale at Macy's Department Store. It isn't going to happen. With both monumental events, you just need to slow down, take your sweet time, and enjoy the ride.

WHEN SHOULD I BEGIN POTTY TRAINING MY CHILD? Paula Spencer, author of *PARENTING Guide to Your Toddler,* writes,

You can cause far more unnecessary frustrations by starting too early than by giving it time. Around 18–24 months- when your child shows several signs of readiness- is a good time to introduce your child to a potty.

I would go a step farther and declare that parents should not even begin to think about the toilet-training process until the child is *at least* two years of age. Again, there are those children who are the exception to the rule and want to potty train sooner. These children should not be discouraged.

Most little girls tend to show readiness earlier than boys. Parents can begin to look for the signs to appear between the ages of two to three years for girls while it seems boys show readiness closer to the ages of three to four years.

Pushing forward the ages by which parents expect potty interest takes the expectation and sense of urgency out of this transition.

The surest way to fail in the potty-training process is exert pressure on your child.

General Signs of Potty-training Readiness:
Generally speaking, these are guidelines that indicate that your child is ready to potty train. Readiness should be viewed as a combination of the following, not just an interest in flushing the potty.

The child may:

- Be aware than he needs to use the potty and can communicate this to you.

- Begin to have a regular cycle for having bowel movements.

- No longer want to wear a diaper or Pull-Up.

- Be dry at night or during naptime.

- Want to imitate Mommy or Daddy going to the potty.

- Have the ability to take his Pull-Up on and off easily.

- Be embarrassed by a full diaper or Pull-Up and insist on a new one that is clean and dry.

- Be curious about using the potty and other bodily functions.

- Ask to use the potty chair or toilet.

- Be celebrating his twenty-fifth birthday… (Got ya!)

Some parents may be overly encouraged when twenty-month-old Jeremy indicates that he wants to sit on the potty. "He must be ready to potty train!" they exclaim. In reality Jeremy is just beginning to show signs of readiness.

It can be difficult to be encouraging without having expectation. Take a deep breath at this point and remind yourself that potty training can be a slow process for some children, one that cannot be rushed without causing serious frustration. This transition should be completely controlled by the child.

REINFORCEMENTS DURING THE POTTY-TRAINING PROCESS

Once the child has been showing readiness signs with more regularity, it is time to begin toilet training. Moms and dads may want to consider different options for positive reinforcement.

Games

Some children respond to this type of potty-training reinforcement very well in that games create a playful environment in which the child can practice her new skill. Games take the fear out of the toilet mystery and replace it with special time with Mommy and Daddy.

Some of the games my children enjoyed were:

1. Cheerios game
    This game involved putting five or six cheerios in the toilet water and allowing the boys to take aim and shoot the Os! They found this activity very amusing. Unfortunately it never did help with their aim!

2. Ride the horsey
    This game involves helping the child (boys and girls) sit backward on the potty as though riding a horse. Children become confident because they can hold onto the back of the toilet. This helps

to eliminate the fear that they will fall in. Some moms and dads even keep a cowboy hat nearby!

3. Relocate the candy jar!

    Some parents find that their children respond to a sweet treat for any attempt at the potty. Place a sealed candy jar that contains small candies on the bathroom counter. This is a tasty reminder to practice! In the beginning, your child may receive a candy just for sitting on the potty. However, as time goes by, she may only get a candy for actually using the toilet. For some children the candy jar is a tempting offer that they just can't refuse! Even *I* will tinkle for a Skittle!

4. Beat the clock!

    This game involves a two-to-four-ounce glass of juice and a kitchen timer. Once the child drinks the glass of juice completely, set the timer for fifteen minutes. The object of the game is to use the potty before the timer rings. If he beats the clock, he gets a piece of candy from the candy jar. For some children, fifteen minutes may not be enough time to be successful. If this is the case, set the timer for twenty minutes the next time.

Big-Girl Panties/Big-Boy Pants

Buying big-girl or big-boy pants can be a big deal to the potty-training child. It is a concrete sign that they are something special and have a new skill to be proud of. In the beginning stages of potty training, you can use big-boy or big-girls pants with the beat the clock game. Put the new pants on the child right before she drinks her juice. Let her practice pulling them up and down. When the urge strikes, her timing, as well as the ability to go quickly, will be an added plus!

Sticker Charts

Behavioral charts can be a very effective way to involve your child in the toilet-training process. The reinforcement is immediate, and for some children, stickers are the next best thing to candy! You can find a wide variety of charts in teacher-supply stores, or you can simply make up your own as we will discuss in Chapter 6.

It is fun for the children to pick out stickers they are interested in. Action-figure stickers may appeal to some boys while ballerina stickers may appeal to the girls.

Bottoms Up!

Some parents prefer to wait until the hot summer months to potty train their children for two reasons:

First, some children have a tough time making the connection between the physical urge to *use* the toilet and the act of actually going *on* the toilet.

In this case, the fewer the clothes to take off, the better. Some moms and dads prefer to allow the children to use Pull-Ups or training pants only during the daylight hours to enhance their chances of success. The fewer the clothes to deal with, the better.

Secondly, by "bottoms up" I am referring to allowing the child to play bare bottomed. Some parents find this method successful because by not wearing underpants, they are cutting out a step, thus allowing the child to concentrate solely on making it to the potty on time. Be prepared for lots of accidents, plan to spend time playing outside, and don't forget your sunscreen!

Of course, there are dozens of games you can play with your child to get them interested in going potty on the toilet. By using your imagination, you can have a playful, positive impact on successfully toilet training your child.

WHAT TO AVOID DURING THE POTTY-TRAINING PROCESS

Watch Your Language!

When parents use words like *stinky, nasty,* or *gross* during the potty training process, the child can begin to feel that going to the toilet in general is *stinky, nasty,* or *gross.*

Two-year-old Scottie has begun to show signs that he is ready to potty train. His mommy is very excited for him because when he can go pee pee and poo poo on the potty, he won't have to wear those "nasty diapers" anymore. He will be a "big boy" then. Scottie is confused because he has always worn diapers for as long as he can remember. Since his mommy started sitting him on the potty chair, his poo poo diapers are "stinky" and should not be in his pants. It seems his mommy is not happy with him for going pee pee in his diaper. Scottie doesn't want to go "stinky poo poo" in his pants or the potty, and he doesn't care if he's a "big boy" either.

It's so important for the child to view this transition as a normal function of life. We talked about games, charts, candy, all the fun reinforcements of potty training, but there is a fine line parents walk while making it entertaining. Moms and dads need to make sure that while they are encouraging the use of the potty, they are not placing guilt on the child for holding on to his old way of doing things.

The best reaction in this case is no reaction. Going to the toilet is as normal as taking out the trash. We're all happy to have the old trash removed and a fresh garbage bag to replace it, but nobody jumps up and down and cheers compulsively when it's gone, and nobody goes on and on about how stinky that bag of trash was (most of the time anyway). The same can be said about going to the potty. Sometimes the less said the better.

Adult Power!

Adult power refers to the struggle that can ensue between moms and dads and the potty training child. Using the toilet is merely one of many steps in the quest to teach the child to be independent. Just as learning to feed themselves is something to be practiced, understanding the concept of using the toilet takes practice as well.

Three-year-old Marcus has decided he does not like the "stupid potty." He doesn't want to wear those ugly big-boy pants, and he could care less about shooting cheerios with his pee pee. His mommy tells him that it's time for him to be a "big boy" now, but he pretends he can't hear her and continues to play with his trucks on the floor. "Don't you want to try to sit on the potty, Marcus? Come on, honey, let's try!" Marcus ignores his mommy because that's all she cares about is that dumb ol' potty. Mommy finally leaves with a disappointed sigh.

It's easy to feel his mommy's frustration. Maybe she is getting pressure from his preschool to have him toilet trained before the fall sessions begin. Maybe she is embarrassed because all of the other three-year-old boys in the playgroup are well on their way to being completely potty trained. She has tried everything, and still he has no interest.

This mommy needs to completely drop the subject of the potty to Marcus. If Marcus wants a diaper, give him the diaper. One thing is for sure: when Marcus is ready to go to the toilet, he will let his mommy know. Only it will be *his* decision. Some children are more strong willed than others, and even though capable, they want to be in control.

Allow them to feel that using the potty is their idea. By giving them control, you eliminate the power issue.

Times of Change

Some moms and dads feel pressure to toilet train their children quickly because they may have a new baby coming, or maybe they are moving to another house and feel that would be one thing less to worry about.

This can cause frustration on both sides by rushing the process.

Monica views her world differently than her mommy and daddy. Her mommy says there is a baby in her tummy. Her tummy is *huge*. She even walks funny. Her daddy says the baby is going to be a new sister for her to play with, but Monica doesn't even know what a sister is.

Lately all mommy and daddy talk about is the new baby, and it gives Monica a stomachache just listening to it. Her mommy says every day, "Monica, you need to learn to go potty on the toilet like a big girl! One day you can teach your baby sister to be big like you." Monica decides she doesn't want this new sister, whatever it is, and she doesn't want to be a big girl either. She just wants things to be the way they used to be.

Change can make children nervous. A new baby is an enormous change for any family but especially young children. Potty training can be a very stressful transition on some children, so if at all possible, keep the number of changes to a minimum.

If your family is moving into a new home, try to wait until your family is settled into their new routine. Some small children relapse and begin wetting the bed again during a move, so you will be saving yourself this added pressure if you put the brakes on introducing any new changes.

Depending on the child's readiness, some parents prefer to wait to potty train their children until they are adjusted to their big-boy -girl beds. This allows for one change at a time and gives the child more time to show signs of wanting to use the toilet on their own.

It is confusing for some young children to absorb a new home, new surroundings, a new member of the family, and a new bed. While these are all positive and exciting changes for any family, they can make some children nervous and uneasy. Take it slowly and allow the child to set the pace.

"Bed-wetting is not deliberate. It is less of a learned skill and more of a physiological development. Nighttime control is largely involuntary," says Vickie Lansky. It is not considered to be a problem until children are six or seven years old by most pediatricians. Some children develop at a different pace than others in their nighttime bladder control.

According to Vicki Lansky, there are many reasons why some children have difficulty staying dry all night. Below are just a few:

1. Some children simply mature physically slower than other children.

2. Parents who wet the bed as adolescents have a 75 percent chance of having children who wet the bed.

3. Some children fall into such a deep sleep that it is difficult to wake up to respond to the urge to urinate during the night.

4. Changes in a child's life such as a new house, sibling, or new school may be factors that contribute to bedwetting.

5. Illnesses such as bladder infections or chronic constipation may trigger bedwetting.

There are many ways to deal with bedwetting, though punishment should never be considered as an option. Three factors offer success for a child who wets the bed:

1. Physical maturity on behalf of the child and patience on behalf of the moms and dads.

2. Medical help if moms and dads suspect the problem is physical or abnormal. There are several medications on the market that are extremely effective with older children. Talk with your doctor to help you make the right choice.

3. Alarm devices that condition a child to learn to wake from their deep sleep when the urge to urinate occurs during the night.

I don't suggest using rewards or charts with night-time bedwetting because it implies that the child has control over the problem. Most children do not. Setting up reinforcements that the child cannot voluntarily obtain is disappointing.

Wake Up!
Signaling devices can be worth their weight in gold for children over six years of age who are still having problems staying dry during the night.

Most of these alarms use the same basic principle. Wet-sensitive sensors are used either in the form of a bed pad or clip that hooks directly to the child's underpants. When the child starts to urinate during the night, the alarm goes off. Over time the child will be conditioned to awaken, by himself, by the urge to urinate.

There are many different companies who supply alarm-signaling devices. The prices for these alarms can range from fifty dollars and higher. Alarm devices can be found through medical-supply companies, pharmaceutical departments, or your medical physician.

While wet-sensitive alarms have a high success rate, they do have some disadvantages:

1. They can be disturbing to some children when they suddenly awaken during the night.

2. Some children sleep through the alarms.

3. Some alarms can wake the entire family, not just the bedwetting child.

4. Some children have a tough time getting back to sleep.

5. Most alarms have to be reset.

GOLDEN RULE

Patience is a virtue.

Or, if you don't like that golden rule, you can use my mother's favorite:

"Relax. Not many teenagers receive their high school diploma wearing a diaper."

That kind of puts it all into perspective.

Now that you've got everyone sleeping through the night, you're organized during the day, and you're on your way to dry underpants, let's move on to helping you overcome those dinner-time blues!

Chow Time! Simple Ways to Feed Your Busy Family

"Hamburgers and french fries again? Aw, c'mon Mom! Can't we have pork roast and spinach just this once?!"

Okay, so this may never happen. But nowadays most families live life in the fast lane. It's easier to go through a drive through than to cook a hot meal.

Whether you are at home with toddlers, watching for the bus for pre-teens, or wondering what you've got in mass quantities in the refrigerator to feed your teenager, mealtime can be a real issue for any mom.

Some moms don't cook, don't like to cook, and have no intentions of ever, ever cooking. But the fact still remains that your family has to eat *something*. I have found that the older children get, the more of a dilemma this becomes.

I have four men to feed every night. My boys are not petite in any way. In fact they seemed to be born wanting pork tenderloins and BBQ ribs.

When I was a little girl, both my parents worked. But my mother made sure that my siblings and I had a hot meal every night. I remember those dinners together vividly. We discussed our days at school, our family business, and our vacation plans. We told jokes and laughed a lot. I guess at some point in my life I wanted to create that warm, fuzzy, memory for my children as well.

Our busy schedules tear us into so many different directions that it's nice to have one special time together, if only for half an hour. Dinnertime isn't just about eating. It's about togetherness as well as nutrition.

Jeannie Ralston, author of *Eat together, Stay Healthy,* in an October 2000 *Ladies Home Journal* article, writes,

The family dinner seems to have fallen victim to our frenzied times. Only 43 percent of families eat together daily, according to a recent study by Harvard Medical School. This is unfortunate because the study, which surveyed 16,000 children aged nine to fourteen, shows that those who ate with their parents frequently had healthier eating habits than those who didn't. Twenty-four percent of kids who dined with their families daily got the recommended five servings of fruits and vegetables, compared with just 13 percent of those who rarely or never ate together. They also ate less fried food and consumed more calcium, fiber, iron and vitamins C and E. "There are two possible explanations," says Matthew W. Gillman, M.D., associate professor of ambulatory care and prevention at Harvard Medical School. "When kids eat with their parents, there may be more nutritious food on the table. Or maybe the dinner conversation includes a discussion about healthful eating."

Studies have also shown that families who eat dinner together have a higher rate of children furthering their education. The correlation could be due to the fact that the family unit takes the time to ask questions about school, how children did on their tests, or what famous American they were planning to write a book report about this week. In short, dinnertime is a time set aside each day to stay involved with one another.

After our family blessing, we each take turns talking. It is a nice feeling to have someone ask you, "So how was your day?" young or old. Though try not to get your feelings hurt when your family isn't quite as excited about those lovely ripe tomatoes you found on sale or the packages you mailed off at the post office.

I spice my life up by telling the boys I'm really an international spy and can't tell them any more information without jeopardizing our mission. They laugh and give me a "Yeah, right, Mom, in your next life!"

This is important conversation! It is the highlight of my day. The meal itself is merely the *draw* that brings us together. The meal *time* is invaluable in terms of quality togetherness. Most children feel a sense of foundation when moms and dads are able to stop the insanity of their lives, come together, and enjoy the closeness of a family meal. Use this time to get to know each other. Our children grow so fast that sometimes it's hard to keep up with who they are becoming. Families can stay connected by making dinnertime together a priority.

Cooking doesn't have to be a dreaded issue. I am going to give you some easy tips to enhance your cooking skills in order to put a hot, nutritious meal before your family every night.

By planning in advance, you accomplish three things:

1. A one-stop shop will save you money!
    You will save yourself a bundle of money at the grocery store by carefully planning your weekly menu and going only once. Keep a list of household items that you run out of on your refrigerator to add to your weekly list. This avoids impulse buying.

2. No last-minute jitters for the chef! (Save this weakness for the shoe department.)
    Decide what meals you plan to make that week and write down on your grocery list everything it will take to make those recipes. This way, when you're ready to make the meal, everything is at your fingertips… No panicking that you've run out of oregano.

3. Take the guessing out of mealtime!
    By planning in advance, you take the four-p.m. what-am-I-going-to-fix-for supper? fear out of your day. Your beef stroganoff is thawing in the refrigerator, and your egg noodles are ready to boil!

4. Run, don't walk, and get yourself a Crock Pot.
   Slow cooking in a Crock Pot is a busy mom's salvation! A Crock Pot is a necessary tool in the mommy business. They are the greatest asset when you plan to be gone all day long with those Saturday soccer games that can go on forever.

   What's helpful with this type of cooking is that the only talent you need is in following a recipe of how to dump ingredients into a pot, cover the lid, and turn it off when it's done. I call this my dump n' run meal. I use several slow-cooker recipe books. They can be a lifesaver and the recipes are delicious!

5. Neighborhood dinner plans.
   We all know the old proverb "it takes a village…" How true! Several of our neighborhood moms participate in a neighborhood dinner plan. This is where each family takes a day of the week and prepares the meal for all participating families. Some moms really get involved in this so that they are only in the kitchen one day a week!

   Each of the meals planned are kid friendly and may include dessert. Such meals might be a large batch of spaghetti with salad and bread, home-made soup, or grilled hamburgers. Each group comes up with their own set of ground rules for food allergies, delivery times, and children's favorites!

   For the moms who don't enjoy cooking but care about the nutrition of their families, this plan is ideal!

When you're unprepared for mealtime and the children are hungry and cranky, it's too easy to get in the car and find fast food. Or even easier yet to order pizza. Try not to get caught in this trap.

Children today need nutritious meals now more than ever. Let's face it: most school lunches are best described as "mystery meat on a stick and fried potatoes." Children are more obese than in any other time in history. There is too much fast, fat-filled food in their diets. Most families need to re-think what's for supper.

By planning your menu in advance, you can have fresh fruits and vegetables washed and ready to serve, not just every night but at snack times as well. This sets up normal healthy eating habits for your family.

As they grow into adults, they will continue with what's normal to them. Moms need to ask themselves, "Is normal for my children going to be fried chicken fingers, french fries, and coke or baked chicken, rice, green beans, and applesauce?"

I know that a lot of families have picky eaters. We had one in our family as well. "No way. I'm not eating that! It's slimy! Who wants to eat something that's *green* anyway? Not me! No way!"

Sound familiar?

But every night at dinner, even though he never touched a single green bean growing up, I continued to put green beans on his plate along with the other things he would like to eat. Then, overnight it seemed, my son grew up, sprouted a beard, and started eating green beans. I am confident it is because it was part of my plan to create healthy, familiar foods that would register as normal to him one day. But it just might have been that after one year of college dormitory cafeteria food, anything I made would have tasted wonderful to him.

Regardless of when my children began their love affair with salads, vegetables, and healthy foods, I like to think it has a little to do with my perseverance in creating a healthy mealtime environment at home.

We all know the old wives' tale that says children will eat when they are hungry.

It's true.

DISCOVER BULK SHOPPING

Shopping in bulk is not exclusively saved for large families. There is a misconception about this type of shopping. By shopping at these warehouses, such as Sam's Club, Costco's, etc., you are not only saving yourself money but time as well.

I buy most of my meats from a warehouse. They come in large quantities packs, and the meats are high quality and less expensive. When I get home I separate them into family portions, wrap the meat in freezer foil, label them, and place them in my deep freezer. One pack of pork chops may end up being three family portions for three separate meals. One package of sixteen chicken breasts may be four family portions, and so on.

They are sold at a cheaper price per pound. Plus, my freezer is filled with chicken, hamburger, pork chops, stew meat, sausage etc., ready for my recipes.

These warehouses also have large bags of frozen vegetables, which are just as nutritious as fresh produce.

To become a member of these warehouses, there is usually an annual fee. Most charge approximately twenty-five to thirty dollars. But it is well worth it with what you will save by purchasing in bulk.

INVEST IN A LARGE FREEZER!

I love my freezer. I love my freezer the way teenagers love Katy Perry… total admiration minus the sky high heels.

It has paid for itself a thousand times over by storing what I've purchased in bulk as well as cooked in bulk. You may not think your family is big enough to justify an additional freezer, but it is an essential part of being organized and having mealtime prepared.

You will be amazed how fast it fills up with economy-size freezer bags of vegetables, spaghetti sauce, chili, beans, meats, chicken, roasts, and, of course, those twenty-four pound cakes you can make in advance at Christmas time to give to housekeepers, teachers, grandparents, mailmen, garbage collectors, tutors, music teachers, and coaches. You *will* fill it up, trust me.

THE GIFT THAT KEEPS ON GIVING: BULK COOKING

Nothing will save your sanity more than bulk cooking. Here's the tricky part. You have to plan for this day. Make arrangements for the children to play at a friend's, do it on the weekends when Daddy can entertain them for a while, or do it during their naptime (not Daddy's). I will, for example, plan to cook after church when I know we're just going to be piddling around the house with no pressing plans.

By "cooking in bulk," I am not only referring to doubling, but sometimes tripling recipes to freeze in family portions for future meals and also cooking meals that are similar in ingredients or require the same amount of time to prepare.

For example, I may be making a meatloaf. But I use basically the same recipe for meatloaf that I use for meatballs for my spaghetti sauce (with the exception of Italian seasonings, etc.) and also for my hamburger patties. (Hey, I never claimed to be a gourmet chef.) So instead of making one meatloaf, I may take three times the amount of hamburger and make three meals to freeze instead of only one.

This way, in the future when I'm wondering what to serve for supper, I can pull from my freezer hamburgers, meatballs for spaghetti, or a meatloaf, and I did it all with one easy preparation.

When I decide to make chicken and sausage gumbo, which my boys love, I always make Cajun red beans and sausage at the same time. Both require sausage and the same amount of time to cook down the ingredients.

If I have to hang around the kitchen for two hours to make gumbo, I might as well use my time wisely and make red beans to serve over rice as well. Both freeze beautifully and yield quite a few meals. It's cost and time effective.

When it's time to refill my freezer with a healthy dose of spaghetti sauce, I make a batch of chili as well. Same basic ingredients, same amount of time to cook down.

Take a small portion of chili, and put it into a smaller storage container and serve your family some chili-dogs as a treat one night!

My whole family loves Mexican food. Once in a while I will make a double batch of taco meat. With one portion I'll serve tacos with a salad. I'll freeze the other portion, and when the Mexican urge hits us again, I use it to make cheese and beef quesadillas on my pancake griddle!

On the weekends, my boys love french toast and pancakes. So if I'm making them, instead of making one batch, I'll make a whole freezer-bag full of each and freeze them for breakfast to pop in the toaster during the school week when they tire of cereal or scrambled eggs. It's also much cheaper than buying frozen pancakes!

FOOD FOR THOUGHT

Once you've decided on when to do your cooking, here are some suggestions of what to do for dinner. I usually choose to make three meals at a time. One to serve and I freeze the other two.

Hamburger
>   Spaghetti meat sauce
>   Baked ziti
>   Meatball sandwiches
>   Grilled hamburgers
>   Tacos
>   Hamburger and rice
>   Chili
>   Meatloaf

Beef quesadillas
Minestrone soup

Grilled or Baked Chicken
Chicken fajitas
Chinese chicken with fried rice
Chicken and sausage jambalaya
Chicken and cheese quesadillas
Chicken, yellow rice, and pea's casserole
Baked potatoes with cheese and chicken topping
Baked chicken with mushroom soup over rice
Chicken noodle soup
Chicken tortilla soup
Grilled chicken salad
Chicken and sausage gumbo
Sliced chicken and veggies
Chicken spaghetti
Chicken tetrazzini

Lean Stew Meat
Beef and vegetable soup
Crock Pot beef stroganoff
Beef tips over rice

These are just a few ways to use your favorite recipes wisely. All of these items freeze well and usually require minimal time during the week to heat up and prepare. By adding fruits, salads, rice, noodles, vegetables, to warm French bread, you can have a hassle-free variety of nutritious meals ready for your family before they can ask, "Mom, what's for supper?"

Warning: Your husband may faint.

By planning your menu, taking advantage of bulk warehouses, buying yourself a new (or used) freezer, and cooking in bulk, you will find you have more time to spend enjoying your family.

Let's move on to how you can help your family develop responsibilities and help you more around the house. (Collect yourself and stop laughing! It can be done!)

The Family Basket: Teaching Your Family Responsibility

"Whadda ya mean, 'Make my bed?'" said the fifteen-year-old to his mother.

"I mean, make your bed. You know, straighten the sheets and comforter." she answered, exasperated.

"C'mon Mom, get real!" he said, sounding confused. "I have to leave in thirty, minutes and I still have to shower!"

Learning to take care of responsibilities is not ever going to be a high priority to a child. Moms and dads have to make it a high priority within the family unit.

Working together as a family allows your children to feel connected to something stable and organized. These foundations will not only give children a sense of accomplishment but will also prepare them to be independent.

So many children today aren't prepared for the outside world. They leave home unable to cope with doing laundry, taking care of their automobiles, much less being able to scramble eggs. By doing everything for the children, parents rob them of the experience of being self-reliant.

Let's say for sixteen years you have picked up Sarah's dirty clothes off of her bedroom floor and washed them for her. One day you decide you've had enough of picking up after Sarah and everyone else in the family. You feel put upon and hurt that no one can see that you could use a little more help around the house. You begin screaming, "I'm not doing this anymore! From now on, you all are picking up after yourselves!"

Sound familiar?

Your children:

A. Say, "You're right, Mom. From now on, we'll take over and give you the rest you deserve!"

B. Say, "Did you say something, Mom?"

C. Laugh hysterically as they grab your car keys and sputter, "Good one, Mom!"

Fortunately or unfortunately, our children are what we teach them at home. Most children cannot learn to be responsible and helpful if they are never taught to be responsible and helpful.

There are several things you can do to involve your children in the daily operation of your home. By following these simple steps, you can ensure that when your children leave your home, they will not scrunch their faces in bewilderment when someone asks them to empty the trash.

Here are three important questions moms and dads can ask themselves before assigning chores to young children:

1. Is Abigail able to fully understand what I've just asked her to do? Instructions must be short and issued in an age-appropriate language.

    Example wrong way: "Abigail, pick up your toys and put them back on the shelf with the books on the bottom shelf and the Barbies on the top shelf." Two-year-old Abigail will only stare at you blankly. Way too much information!

    Right way: "Abigail, let's play clean up!" Then proceed to show, by example, what "playing clean up" means. Repetition will teach Abigail that the Barbies belong on the top shelf.

2. Are the responsibilities I'm giving Andy *age appropriate?* As much as you'd like him to, three-year-old Andy is not going to be able to unload the dishwasher without a disaster here or there.

3. Are the jobs I'm giving Emma fun, or am I barking orders?

4. By making chores game-like, mommies can make being responsible more enjoyable for all involved.

    • Turn some music on and have the children freeze when you mute it as they pick up their action figures.

    • Dance with your child as you show her how to put her stuffed animals back on the shelf.

    • Have a race to see who can pick up the most blocks and put them back into the bucket.

Two to Three Years Old

By the ages of two to three years, children are able to understand simple instruction. Suggested responsibilities for two- to three-year-olds are:

- Picking up toys in the family room and placing them in the toy bucket.

- Helping Mommy water the plants outside.

- Helping Mommy with emptying the hamper by putting all of the white clothes in one pile, the red clothes in another pile, etc. (Helps with learning their colors too!)

- Help Mommy and Daddy wash the car. Reality: you will wash the car, and they will have a ball playing with the garden hose and later on tell tall tales to Grandma of how they washed daddy's car that day.

Four to Five Years Old

By the time a child is four to five years old, most children should be responsible for:

- Making her/his bed.

- Getting dressed by himself/herself.

- Brushing his/her teeth after breakfast and before bedtime.

- Feeding the family pet if parents make the food easily available.

- He/she should be able to bring dishes to the sink after a meal.

Remember, it's important to help your children be successful. Show them how to do the chore that you are asking them to do and praise their work. A child's best with making her bed may be worlds apart from your idea of a made-up bed.

In these early stages of teaching children, mommies and daddies may want to concentrate on a great attitude about doing the job more than the job itself.

Six and Seven Years Old

By the ages of six and seven years old, your children can begin chores such as:

- Dusting.
- Emptying small trash cans.
- Helping to clean the dinner table off with a sponge.
- Cleaning windows.
- Sweeping floors.
- Wiping off the bathroom sinks.
- Helping organize their play areas.
- Helping clean out the garage by moving bicycles, etc., and sweeping once it's cleared.
- Helping pull weeds in the garden and rake leaves.
- Vacuuming carpets.

Eight to Nine Years Old

In addition to other learned responsibilities, most eight- and nine-year-olds are ready to help out with some new chores such as:

- Sorting out laundry.

- Replacing buttons on a shirt.

- Loading/unloading the dishwasher.

Ten to Eleven Years Old

By ten and eleven years of age, some children can:

- Help Dad mow the lawn and other yard work with careful supervision.

- Wash and vacuum the car and help Dad check the fluid levels in the engine and air pressure in the tires.

- Help do the laundry, fold clothes, and put away.

- Change bed sheets.

- Do supervised cooking.

- Help Dad with simple repairs like replacing a toilet seat, hanging pictures, and fixing bicycles.

Twelve to Thirteen Years Old

At twelve and thirteen years of age, if carefully encouraged, children can be knowledgeable of so many things! This might be the age, depending on maturity, that you allow your pre-teen to baby-sit for younger siblings.

I suggest two things in order to make babysitting a successful experience for all involved:

1. Pay your pre-teen!
    Socially, pre-teens begin to have invitations to do so many things. By babysitting, Jordan is able to make some extra spending money to splurge on those video games!

2. Pay his younger siblings to follow the directions of your pre-teen!
    Figure out what you would have paid a regular babysitter. Give half to your pre-teen, and the other half I suggest splitting between the younger siblings. If a sibling is too young to appreciate money as a dangling carrot for good behavior, offer a lollipop, special movie, or other such incentives.

Now that you are aware of the benefits of starting early, and some age-appropriate suggested chores, we will continue on so that you can learn how to get them to do all of these wonderful jobs around the house.

THE POT OF GOLD AT THE END OF THE RAINBOW
Now, I know I've got you breathing heavy at the mere notion of your children helping out with all of the chores I

listed previously. Most children *can* do these chores. Now, the secret is to get them to *want* to do these chores.

By having a pot of gold at the end of the rainbow, I am referring to the basic childhood mentality... "What's in it for me?"

Your two-year-old's pot of gold may be that when she's finished picking up her toys and putting them on the shelf, you tickle her, squealing "Good job, sweetie pie!"

For a four-year-old who is learning to tie his shoes by himself, his pot of gold may be a movie rental and home-made popcorn when he finally ties them without your help.

For your ten-year-old, his pot of gold may be that if he cleans out the garage and helps dad with the yard on Saturday, you'll take him to go to the roller skating rink with a friend.

But whatever pot of gold you use, make sure that it is only acquired by doing the chores with a good attitude, in a timely manner, and to the best of their ability. It's important to teach them that good effort is rewarded.

Allowance

Some parents may want to use allowance. I support allowance for children, particularly when they have a standard set of chores they are responsible for during the week.

Again, attitude, timely manner, and doing these chores to the best of their ability should count toward their pay off.

I give allowance for making their beds, getting dressed, feeding the dog, brushing their teeth, and remembering to turn off their lights before going to the bus stop.

(Everyone in our family is responsible for helping to keep the electric bill down each month. With what we save each month, we may use to go get ice cream or go the movies.)

My boys are also responsible for doing their homework in the afternoon and helping with family day on the weekend.

They know what is expected during the week, and after years of reminding them, there is no discussion about what to do. They go about their normal routines without my saying a word… Well, most of the time. (Who am I kidding?)

In keeping with the pot-of-gold theory, allowance doesn't mean a thing if they don't *need* the money. If you give them five dollars every time they are invited to the movies, children won't need their own money, thus negating the motivation of something to work toward.

Moms and dads who choose to give children allowance may need to make sure that the children are old enough to appreciate monetary pot-of-gold payoffs. It's important to note that most children would much rather have your time than money.

Establish a Routine and Be Consistent

Have you ever asked yourself, "How does Johnny's teacher get him to do all of this work?" Well, Johnny's teacher has established what is expected of him from his very first day at school.

Mrs. Carlson puts a *what's-expected routine* into place and provides reinforcement for Johnny's good behavior. Each day her curriculum may change slightly, but Johnny knows his school-work requirements and is comfortable and secure with what's expected.

Johnny's home life shouldn't be any different. If Mommy and Daddy do not teach children a family routine of what's expected, then certainly they will never rise to that ability.

It takes careful planning and patient teaching, but most children can learn age-appropriate chores if taught.

The flip side of the pot of gold for not doing your chores may result in undesirable consequences.

If Susan didn't make her bed that morning, then maybe she needs to miss out on playing with her friend that afternoon. Responsibilities are to be taken care of first; then you may play. It won't take Susan long to learn that making her bed in the morning is part of her routine and must be taken care of each day before she leaves for school.

We started a new consequence recently for leaving your bedroom light on in the morning… fifty cents docked from your weekly allowance.

My boys also know that if you can't get out of bed in the morning and get dressed on time to catch the bus with a good attitude, then maybe you need to go to bed an hour earlier than the other siblings who did have a good attitude and did dress on time. This way you'll have plenty of rest in order to wake up nicely the next morning.

Being firm and consistent is essential during this phase.

It's important to let the children know what is expected of them each day. Children need to fully understand the ground rules before suffering consequences.

As with any new routine within your family, it is so important to praise them constantly for doing well. We give lots of hugs and let them know just how much their participation is appreciated. Again, they want to please you, so give them the chance to make you proud.

Behavioral Sticker Charts

Charts can be extremely effective for smaller children ages three to eight. They love these visual incentives. You can use them for anything from going potty to helping to bring in the groceries from the car. Young children love to see their progress and play with stickers. A chart full of stickers is concrete evidence that they are good children and that they have pleased you.

My only problems with the store-bought behavioral charts are:

- They are expensive, and if you have more than one child, it can be too much to buy one for everyone.

- They are limiting to what you are expecting from your child. Store-bought charts usually don't have as part of their lists "good listener," "nice to my brother," "shared with my friend," "helped my mommy nicely," etc.

When I was looking for my behavior charts, I tried to find a chart individually tailored for the age level of each of my children.

Good behavior should be reinforced immediately. Sometimes it is not convenient for me to stop what I'm doing and help the children put their sticker in the proper place on their charts. Therefore, I found I was letting good behavior slip by because I couldn't stop stirring the scrambled eggs or comforting a hysterical sibling to help the boys reward themselves.

Store-bought charts all have their benefits, and I do agree that the children love them, so I came up with my own chart. It's simple, cost effective, incorporates the stickers they love, and it's accessible to them anytime I catch them being good.

By hanging their behavior charts just below the captain calendar, located in my kitchen, the boys have complete control over tracking their good behavior.

Each Sunday, we start over. I give each child a fresh piece of typing paper. They decorate it, write their names at the top, and hang it on the bulletin board with a brightly colored tack.

We have dozens of stickers to choose from hanging next to their charts. There are no good-behavior categories. There are no boxes to squeeze your favorite sticker into. The children can place the stickers anywhere they please on their papers!

The sky is the limit for what I catch them being good at. This way, if I am busy burning a roast and my six-year-old tells me that he just learned how to change the toilet paper roll, I can say, "Give yourself a sticker! I'm so proud of you for trying something new that can help me out so much!" They love this.

The secret to this chart method being successful is the goal. Our goal is posted with our charts in full view on our bulletin board as a daily reminder of what we are working for. When we make our charts, we all decide what we're working for that week. Depending on the ages of your children, your goal may look something like this:

Weekly Goal for Randy!

    20 stickers = a package of water balloons

    30 stickers = an Icee with a friend on Saturday

    40 stickers = a family picnic in the park on Saturday

    50 stickers = having a friend over for pizza and a rented movie.

Mommies can help the children be as creative as they would like to be! Try to make sure that your goal is not only age appropriate but also fitting with their pot-of-gold desires.

Be careful not to go overboard with your goal charts, or you may have trouble topping it each week, and the incentive may wane after a few weeks.

Family Day!

Family day is a designated weekend day that moms and dads can set aside to work as a family. This day is designed to take care of general maintenance around the house such as cleaning out the garage, weeding the garden, mopping the floor, cleaning the bathrooms, folding laundry, dusting, vacuuming, and washing windows.

When parents plan a family day, here are some important things to consider:

- Make sure that the children are aware of this day in advance. This prevents possible melt downs for some children who may have had a different idea of how they intended to spend their Saturday morning.

- Try to make sure that all family members are present and there are no conflicting baseball games, confirmed birthday parties, or recitals.

- Be efficient. Parents should have a written list of what they need accomplished that morning. We give each of our children a to-do list. This allows the children to work smart. The child that chooses to have a bad attitude about his chores shouldn't have to hold up the progress for those who are willing to do their work nicely, finish their chores, and go out to play.

- Moms and dads need to have the tools necessary available for each chore. If parents want help washing windows, have the cleaner available. No need to frustrate the children while running to the store to purchase more.

- Some parents may want to end their family work day with a fun activity such as a family basketball game, or a bike ride together.

- Praise your children for their help and let them know how much you appreciated their work and their good attitudes.

One of the things that I like best about this day is not only do you get to spend some quality time with your children to teach them new skills, but it promotes a sense of family togetherness.

Remember, chores, like anything in life, are only as fun and interesting as you make it. This is a great ritual to introduce to your family to get things done around the house.

The Family Basket

By far this has been the most effective method I've used with my children because it is fun!

The family basket is something my mother created when we were young, and I remember then how much I looked forward to playing this game. It consists of a small, wicker basket, sissors and a piece of plain, white paper. I take an of inventory of what needs to be done: trash cans emptied, family room dusted, toys picked up in the game room, sheets changed, etc. I write each individual chore down on the typing paper and cut them out. I fold each chore up and put them all in my wicker basket. As each chore is completed, they run back to the basket for their next pick. Each child picks the same amount of chores.

Children can work at their own pace, and the first one finished is the winner! We make it a big deal and chuckle when one of them draws a chore that is yucky such as swishing out the guest bathroom toilet. By making it a game, they are hardly aware that they are learning important tasks.

This method works especially well for younger children who may need chore time to be fun and game oriented.

As a note, moms and dads may need to be very precise with chores with this game. To say to a young child, "Clean the game room," may be too overwhelming. Divide what needs to be done in the game room into several chores, such as pick up all of the blocks, pick up the stuffed animals, and put all of the Barbies back on the shelf. Don't set them up for failure by being too general and expecting too much.

Start Early!

Some parents with teenagers are puzzled at the lack of control they have over their children. Their teenagers borrow their car only to have it returned filthy, full of food wrappers, and on empty. The children beg for seventy-five-dollar jeans and leave them on the floor of their bedrooms for weeks at a time. Some teenagers wouldn't know how to push, much less start, a lawn mower. If this is your situation, I understand how difficult it is to digest that your family might need a little help in this area. Keep in mind that motherhood is not a perfect profession, and we all have areas that require improvement.

From the beginning of time, teenagers have been a handful. It isn't that they are bad children; it's just that the teenagers who are disrespectful with others and/or property haven't been taught the discipline and responsibility necessary so that they don't drive you *crazy*.

Parents should never give up on teaching a child these qualities at any age, but there are some direct advantages to starting early. Mainly it's a little difficult to show Martin how to sort the laundry between football practice, phone calls, and shoveling double-decker bologna sandwiches in his mouth on his never-ending quest to register full.

Most teenagers' attention spans for moms and dads is, well... Let's be honest. There isn't an attention span for moms and dads. So teaching a teenager this late in the game is going to be a little more difficult. Not impossible. Just a little more difficult. "Whatever!" comes to mind.

Again, it is never too late to teach your children.

First, if your teenager needs guidance in the areas of responsibility and respectfulness, *talk to him*. Your teenager is a budding adult with a powerful mind. When you talk to him in a respectful manner about your reasons for *why* it's so important to take care of your vehicle, *why* you need his help around the house, *why* you need him to act respectfully, it can make all the difference. Teenagers, with their rampant hormones, are at times bodies of perpetual frustration. They are growing up and confused as to whether they are young men or still little boys. The most noticeable signal to our children that they are now young adults is when we treat them like young adults. And when they feel like young adults, they tend to act less like children.

Secondly, as parents we have the power to persuade our teenagers to conform to a more civil way to coexist because we have certain items that our teenagers require. Most note-worthy:

1. An automobile

2. Money

For starters, controlling these two items alone should do it for most teens.

Clear rules and responsibilities should be discussed, and adult behavior should be rewarded. We all want to be respected. Teenagers are no different. Tell him how it makes you feel to see the car filled with fast-food wrappers when you've worked so hard to buy a family vehicle. Explain how you need help mowing the grass because you can't afford to pay someone without deducting the amount of money you're saving to send him to college.

Sometimes the biggest issue is that your teenager simply wants to know *why*. So sit down and talk to him … He just might surprise you.

Now that we've discussed how the children can help you with chores around the house and become more independent and responsible, you are ready to learn about some fun, new ways to enjoy your children! Remember, moms and dads, responsibility before play! Thus the order of this chapter on discipline and the next chapter which focuses on *fun!*

By starting early, being responsible becomes a way of life for the children. A two-year-old can pick up her toys in the family room before Daddy comes home from work by making it a game!

When you raise your children from the beginning to know that they are part of a family unit who works together as well as plays together, it becomes a natural part of their everyday lives.

Children want to please us. They want to learn from us. So give them the opportunity to please you! Help them feel the tinge of excitement of a job well done!

Also, by starting young, mommies can avoid having their children grow into teenagers who don't understand the pride of finishing a task.

Responsibility is not something you can rush. It's a gift that is taught slowly over a long period of time, and it will spill over into virtually every aspect of their adult lives.

Something to consider: undisciplined children can be frustrating to their parents, but even more unfortunate is that undisciplined children can grow into undisciplined adults.

The Power of Pancakes: Creative Ways to Enjoy Your Children

"Mommy, I want a stegosaurus!" cheered my middle son. "Hooray for stegosaurus!"

"I'll take a T-rex with great, big teeth!" said my oldest, clapping his hands together.

"I want the dinosaur with the sharp horns on his head! You know, the tri-sir-top dinosaur!" shouted my youngest.

"Three, big, scary dinosaur pancakes coming right up!" I sang from in front of my kitchen griddle.

Making things fun for your family is the best part of parenting. I learned early on as a mommy to be creative or bust! By being creative, parents can achieve two things for their children:

1. By example, mommies can inspire their children to use their own imaginations.

2. Parents can create a healthy balance between fun times and what's expected of them.

I have several ideas for you to experiment with your own children. These are all activities I have done with my children. These projects don't require a lot of time to set up or money. But they are pure fun! Enjoy!

PANCAKE POWER!

You will need:

- Turkey baster
- Pancake mix
- Pancake griddle
- Food coloring
- Raisins/chocolate-chips/whipped topping/ M&M candies.

Use your turkey baster to suck up the pancake mix, and you can create some pretty cool pancakes! Mix your batter with some orange food coloring to make Halloween pumpkins with raisin eyes, nose, and mouth.

At Christmas, mix pancakes with green or red coloring and pour pancake mix into metal Christmas cookie cutters. You can make Christmas trees with ornaments made of M&M candies, snowmen, stars, even Santa himself with whipped topping from a squirt can for the white fur on his hat!

When my boys were toddlers, I would use my turkey baster to spell out their names with the pancake batter. They learned their letters, numbers, shapes, colors, and even our phone number with our morning flapjacks!

Of course, they added their own imaginations to the meal. Chris wanted to learn how to spell his brother's name so he could tell his daddy that night, "Daddy, I ate Josh for breakfast this morning!"

We learned the names of dinosaurs and the planets. It's great fun to eat be able to eat Saturn and Venus all in one sitting!

Pancakes can be a lot of fun, especially when you bypass the fork. Finger pancakes are the best! Even today, my table and chairs are held together by dried syrup from this phase of our lives... so when people come to our house for dinner, they usually stick around.

MOVIE PAJAMA NIGHT

This is for mommies and children alike. Whenever a new children's movie came out on video, I would rush to the video store to rent it. The boys and I would call five or six of our friends and invite them to our house to watch the movie in pajamas. Even the mommies were required to wear their pajamas!

Each child brought their own sleeping bag and pillow. The movie always started after dinner and bath time, so when the movie was over, the children were all ready for bed. We cleared the floor of coffee tables and pushed chairs out of the way, put all the sleeping bags out, and turned off all the lights. It was like a miniature movie theatre. We even served popcorn and Kool-Aid at intermission.

While the children watched the movie, the mommies eat at the dining room table with candles burning, eating munchies that they all brought from home. Even now, with the boys being older, we still have movie night... Of course, none of us wear our pajamas. It's just not cool anymore.

Movie night is a simple occasion to put together and well worth pulling out your flannel pajamas. It's also a whole lot of fun to see what your friends call sleepwear... Things sure have changed with the birth of our children!

RUB A DUB DUB ... A STORY FOR THE TUB!

This is the cure for those evening meltdowns when it's time for a bath. "I don't wanna take a bath!" suddenly turns into, "Hey, Mom! Isn't it time to take a bath?!" The remedy is simple.

Pick out a couple of their favorite books. Let the children get in a tub filled with bubbles. Once submerged, light some candles and turn the lights off. Make sure, of course, the candles are not anywhere near the tub or children. I used to place them on the sink where I could read their stories by candlelight or flashlight. Sometimes we would make up our own stories. Some were funny ones, sometimes scary! While I read, they washed up. This was always a favorite and seemed to wind the children down from a busy day.

By the way, keep the candles in the bathroom, and once you get the children off to sleep, jump in yourself!

ALFRED THE INVISIBLE MOUSE

Some people have imaginary friends. We had an invisible mouse. Yes, a mouse! Alfred came to visit our house once a week. He was a cute little mouse. We knew this because we used to sit at the table and draw pictures of what we thought he looked like. Of course, none of us had ever seen Alfred. But we knew he was there!

Alfred liked to play a game called *Can you learn this in one week?* Each week while we were sleeping, Alfred came to our house and placed whatever letter, shape, color, or number that he wanted us to learn, all over the house.

For instance, if he wanted us to learn the number four, the color blue, and the shape of a diamond that week, he would place papers everywhere the boys were going to be with a blue number four inside the shape of a diamond.

Always at their eye level, the papers were located on the refrigerator, hanging off of the TV, on the mirror by their toothbrushes, and on the closet where they put on their shoes. One paper might be on their toy box or even taped to the ladder to their slide outside.

The rule was every time they saw one of Alfred's signs, the boys had to say "Blue, diamond, number four!" By the end of the week, the boys knew what Alfred had sent them to learn. He always sent a special letter telling them how proud he was and that he had heard them practicing all week. Usually he left a tootsie roll or a lollipop for each child along with his letter.

I cannot tell you how much this helped the boys with learning their letters, numbers, shapes, etc. In fact, by the time they were three years old, not only did they know them all, but they knew the phonetic sounds for each letter as well. They began reading books by themselves by the age of four. Thanks to our invisible mouse, Alfred!

This is a fun game for all involved... Just don't forget to remind Alfred to write his letter and leave the lollipops on the designated day, or you will have a house full of disappointed little ones! They really look forward to his visits!

GIRLS' NIGHT OUT

For those of you with little girls, this is so much fun. It makes you want to be ten again!

When my stepdaughter, Kellie, used to come visit us in the summer, I always tried to do things that appealed to her. One particular visit, we had a slumber party for Kellie and her girlfriends. I got permission from their families first to do glamour shots of the girls with an instant camera during their stay.

Each girl brought a beach outfit, a sports outfit, jeans, and white T-shirt. We did our photo shoots in stages.

While my husband took care of the boys, the girls had a ball in my bathroom getting ready. I curled their hair, put makeup on each one of them, let them cruise through my costume jewelry and long dresses. We painted toenails and fingernails.

We took pictures in our backyard sandbox with their beach outfits. They played on the swing set for their pictures dressed in their sports outfit and even built a human pyramid for their jeans and T-shirt outfits.

Then it was inside for the true glamour. I taped a big sheet on the wall and took pictures of the girls dressed in my costume diamond earrings and some old long dresses that still hung my closet.

Kellie and her girlfriends looked so grown up and glamorous! (Her dad nearly had a heart attack when he saw her in makeup! I had to calm him by telling him we were just playing dress up ... Men!)

It was precious to see these little girls, who were on the fence about whether they were little girls or young ladies, see themselves as pretty for the very first time.

When they left, I gave each of them a booklet with their pictures in them to show their families, friends, neighbors, and whoever else they wanted to brag to in the vicinity.

It was exhausting work, I have to tell you, but even now, I look back at those pictures, and it warms my heart at how much those girls giggled and laughed. It was a wonderful experience that no mother should miss out on.

DIGGING FOR DINOSAUR BONES

When my boys were ages three to five, anything to do with dinosaur bones was a real adventure! Thus the creation of digging for dinosaur bones.

Each night I would sneak out into the backyard and bury large dog biscuits into the sandbox and flowerbeds after we would put the kids to bed.

The next day as soon as breakfast was wolfed down, the boys and I would read a book about dinosaurs and talk about which bones we might discover. I gave them each a bucket and small shovel, and out they went to excavate my dinosaur bones.

Imagination had taken over.

By the time they came in the house, the boys were hungry, thirsty, and ready to share what they had found. Each day brought amazing new discoveries. Word soon caught on that there were dinosaur bones in my backyard, and before I knew it, I had half the neighborhood digging for bones. It's a great exercise for imagination, not to mention all the laundry you can fold while they dig!

WELCOME TO MY DRIVEWAY

During the fall and spring months, our driveway became another world.

The boys and I would create an underwater world, complete with King Neptune, octopuses, sharks, and jellyfish floating in the waters of a sparkling blue sea, or maybe an outer space odyssey filled with meteors and space ships and planets such as Venus and Saturn. Or maybe a picturesque scene with mountains, goats, and little flowers in the meadows below. This was what we talked about before we tackled our driveway with our sidewalk chalk.

We would work on our project for days at a time. Usually I would draw what they wanted me to create, and the children would color it in. Sometimes they would create their own.

The boys learned about which kinds of fish were in the ocean and what planets needed to be in our solar system to be complete. By the time we were finished, we were submerged in our driveway world. It was a marvelous way to spend a lazy afternoon with the boys.

Of course, before starting this project, check your weather channels for your forecast. Raining on this parade before you've finished would be worse than a sandcastle being swept away by a wave!

PLAY-DOH CARTOON CHARACTERS

Play-Doh is always a guaranteed success with children, but sometimes they need a little guidance to help jumpstart their imaginations.

Once they grew tired of the cookie cutters, we came up with new themes to work with, such as who can make the best ice cream cone or the spookiest Halloween mask. Or, for the girls, fake fingernails.

We made space ships and weird-looking aliens, but by far, the most fun was to try to copy our favorite cartoon characters. This always brought a lot of laughs.

When the boys got older, they thought Play-Doh was for babies. But every once in a while, I still bring it down from the shelf and challenge them to a favorite cartoon character party from the *SpongeBob SquarePants* cartoon, or even Bart Simpson.

When presented the right way, older children still have a wonderful time digging into it.

I have found over the years that making your own Play-Doh is not only easier to work with and cheaper than store bought, but it also lasts longer, so I've included it for you. Happy sculpting!

Homemade Play-Doh

1 cup of white flour

¼ cup salt

2 Tbsp of cream of tartar

1 cup of water

2 tsp vegetable coloring

1 tbsp oil

Mix the dry ingredients together
in a large, clean bowl.

Add water, vegetable coloring, and oil.

Transfer to a saucepan.

Cook over medium heat until it sticks together.

Let cool on a clean cutting board.

Knead together until desired consistency.

GAME DAY

Game Day is an event that our entire neighborhood looks forward to each summer. It's become a sort of holiday for us! I started doing this when the children were small, out of desperation to occupy them during the summer months when I had completely run out of ideas.

The general idea is to call the mommies in your neighborhood who seem to be as desperate as you are to find something to do with the kids. Agree upon the best date for everyone. Ask each mom if she would be willing to host a game at their home for thirty minutes that day. That is their only obligation to Game Day. I usually set up the Game Day schedule to start after lunch.

Some of the games we have had success with include:

- Red Rover in the sprinklers
- Pictionary in the garage
- Scavenger hunts
- Water balloon tosses
- Piñatas filled with candy
- Pin the tail on the donkey
- Slip n' Slide with water guns
- Musical chairs
- Volley ball
- Three-legged races
- Bean bag toss
- Pillow case races
- Relay races holding an egg on a spoon
- Toilet paper wraps (Each team races to wrap their captain with TP. The first team to use the whole roll is the winner.)
- Obstacle courses

One particular year we had twenty-two neighborhood children participating! The children were excited, but so were the mommies! I volunteered to stay with the children the whole afternoon as we went from one house to another playing games.

Most mommies like Game Day. When they finish hosting their thirty-minute game, moms can take a nap, read a book, go to the grocery store, clean out their refrigerator, and enjoy the peace and quiet because the children and I are off to the next house!

Usually each mommy has lemonade/Kool-Aid or popsicles because the summer months can be so hot. After the last house, it's usually close to dinnertime. The children run back to their own homes to change clothes and get cleaned up.

Then each of the families meet at the local neighborhood pool with all the children, and we order pizza. This gives us all a chance to visit with each other, and the dads get a chance to swim with the kids.

The effort Game Day takes to put together is minimal, but the rewards are immeasurable. It's truly a day we all looked forward to and the kids had a wonderful time.

NO-TROUBLES BUBBLES

Of course, activity lists would not be complete without the recipe for bubbles! Again, store-bought bubbles are fine, but they don't seem to take shape and last as long as the ones you can make for yourself. It also makes a ton of bubbles, so be prepared for bubbles, bubbles, bubbles!

Homemade Bubbles

1 clean pail

1 cup of Joy, clear Ivory, or green Dawn dish soap

3–4 Tbsp glycerin (any pharmacy)

10 cups of cold water

Mix together well.

Skim the froth off the top and start blowing!

(Twist used hangers from your closet together to use as bubble wands)

Here are a few more Executive Mom ideas to maximize the fun you have with your children:

Play freeze tag with the garden hose

Create sand art pictures

Collect different colored fall leaves and iron them between wax paper

Host dance contests

Dine in a tent in your backyard

Build a dam on rainy days with leaves, rocks, and sand in your street gutters.

Build obstacle courses in your backyard

Write secret messages on typing paper with lemon juice. Just use a warm iron to do the detective work for you!

The list is endless if you use *your* imagination. Not only is it fun for the children, but it's an added bonus for the at-home mom to get to be a child again herself. So in the hustle and bustle of raising your children, don't forget to get down, get dirty, and enjoy them. It's one of the best perks of our job!

Fun, fun, fun! It's easy for mommies to enjoy their children. Now let's talk about a healthy balance between fun and good behavior. Like my dad always said, you never get somethin' for nothin'!

A Balancing Act: Balancing Love and Discipline

Suppose your thirteen-year-old son, Jason, is invited to his best friend, Stanley's party Saturday night. He is extremely pumped up about this event, and you are delighted to see him so excited. Jason, however, has forgotten to mention that Stanley's parents are out of town, and only his seventeen-year-old brother will be home to chaperone.

You find out the truth from your neighbor. When you tell Jason he cannot go without an adult present, he screams, "You don't trust me! You hate me!" And, of course, "You're just trying to ruin my life!" He proceeds to slam doors. Jason is obviously frustrated and angry.

You don't want him to feel like you don't trust him, but you don't want him to go either. This is one of the gray areas of raising children.

In reality, I have found there are more situations with my children that are questionable than are black and white. I am still learning as I go. The truth is I find I get myself into more trouble with my decisions when I second guess myself.

Of course, Jason should not be allowed to go to the party without an adult present. However, the solution to this gray-area situation can be clouded by our overwhelming desire to see our children happy.

Hence the balancing act. How can we manage to make sure our children are happy and yet out of harm's way? Trustworthy yet protected? Hardworking and responsible yet able to understand the importance of playtime? It's quite an obstacle to negotiate!

Years ago—before the age of the permissive parent—mothers, fathers, law officials, and teachers were respected. There was no doubt about the pecking order within the family or schools. There was no tolerance for back talk, lack of self-control, or damage to personal property. To a child there was no mystery over who was in charge.

Today, some moms and dads appear to be afraid of breaking the spirit of a child. Somehow, we have outsourced our core values into believing Jane should be allowed to shatter a lamp when frustrated because she was expressing her anger. Too often there is no consequence for the child who can't keep his hands to himself or bullies other children in school. Some young people believe they are entitled to destroy priceless buildings and bridges with graffiti because they feel they have a right to express their creativity or their inner frustrations.

Mothers and fathers must regain control. We can try to blame the undesirable behavior of our youth on the school system, the government, or hormones. Because ultimately good behavior and respect begins and ends at home.

Licensed psychologist and author of *Dare to Discipline*, Dr. James Dobson responds to parents who believe that children do not need direction and discipline in order to become responsible adults:

> I believe that if it is desirable for children to be kind, appreciative, and pleasant, those qualities should be taught, not hoped for. If we want to see honesty, truthfulness and unselfishness in our offspring, then these characteristics should be the conscious objectives of our early instructional process. If it is important to produce respectful, responsible young citizens, then we should set out to mold them accordingly. The point is obvious: heredity does not equip a child with proper attitudes; children learn what they are taught. We cannot expect the coveted behavior to appear magically if we have not done our early homework.

Our society as a whole changed in the seventies. We began with the career years, which included the me-me-me years, and somewhere in between we established the can't-say-no-to-our-children years. Frankly, folks, it has caused a whole lot of trouble not just for families but for our entire culture as well.

We, as parents, are sodden with guilt. We want our children to have the newest and most sought-after video game systems. We will drive to thirty-five stores to make sure they have it first. Some moms and dads feel it is mandatory that Louise have the most elaborate and form-fitting gown for the prom. Some want their children to be popular and well liked at all costs. Regardless of the inconvenience, some parents want to make sure their children have everything they need to stand out and be recognized.

But what are we really teaching them? Are our children *not* special because they don't have the most fashionable clothes? Is it not possible for them to stand out and be recognized by a natural talent or achieving a goal? As parents, are we sending mixed signals about the importance of being unique, or is being popular in a particular peer group what is being emphasized?

Providing everything for children robs them of the chance to feel the pride of earning the materials themselves.

When a child forgets to take his homework assignments to school, we feel it's unthinkable to allow him to receive a mark for not being responsible. Consequently, some parents will get in the car and take it to school.

Too often we help our children out of jams to a fault. It is painful for any loving parent to permit their child to fail. Yet I have found that failure is one of the most important lessons we can teach them.

By encouraging your child to be honest, respectful, on time, trustworthy, responsible, decent, and hardworking, you are giving them a gift far more long lasting than any toy, dress, or game. These gifts are for a lifetime. Give them the tools they will need to be productive, accountable, and reliable adults. This contribution to their lives requires stamina, courage, and backbone.

Moms and dads do not have to endure back talk, ungratefulness, tardiness, disrespect of property, or lack of control. These behaviors are merely bad habits that need reforming. Children should understand their boundaries and limitations. The sky is not the limit for our children, and this will continue to be the case as long as we live in a civilized society.

To have no boundaries, to be so free and out of control, makes children restless and uneasy. Their personal confidence comes from a foundation of knowing that there is a greater strength than their own watching out for them. This strength is a not a net to catch them, rather a wall to bounce off of as they learn their way.

Parents can't save children from having to abide by rules. As adults there are serious consequences to suffer by not following the rules of society. If you are unfaithful, you may lose your wife. If you are not on time, you may lose your job. If you are dishonest, you may lose your friend. As parents, we are the building blocks for this universal understanding.

Self-reliant, secure, and disciplined children make successful adults. But how do we get them there? Trial and error is a consideration, as some forms of discipline work better on one type of child than another.

Strong-willed children may require a narrower boundary to feel secure while others may accept limitations willingly. It is important to recognize each child for their uniqueness and design your expectations accordingly.

The following ideas have proven successful for my children:

One of the best ways of teaching our children is by example. Four-year-old Mickey is watching you very carefully. He notices how you handle frustration and how you deal with others and will even begin to mimic your conversations with your sister on the phone. He may be a little person, but he is constantly picking up cues from you as to how a big person should behave.

Margie is watching her mommy and daddy have an argument. She may notice that their voices are loud and scary. In the heat of an argument, we are emotionally on edge, and tempers flare. Children get their signals about how grownup husbands and wives behave when frustrated. These are the times when being a copy cat can be scarring if you are not aware of how your children see you. It's important for them to know that it's okay to disagree. But they also need to know how to handle a disagreement properly.

Children will imitate sarcasm, dishonesty, and poor organizational habits. If parents are constantly out of sorts, chances are extremely high that the child will be out of sorts as well, mostly because the child sees this as normal behavior.

If they are taught truthfulness and honesty because you are honest with them, they will grow to value the truth. If they are taught that being on time is important, so important that you yourself are on time for appointments, being on time will be highly regarded.

Children look to us not just for our words; they need to see the action of our words. They need to visualize that being organized and taking care of property, whether personal or otherwise, is a precious asset.

The first and most impressive positive step toward the discipline of any child is for moms and dads to be the role models they are expecting of their children. Remember, small eyes are on you constantly.

POTTY BREAK, AKA TIME OUT

Time out by definition is the act of isolating the child when an *understood* rule has been broken. It is an effective way to deal with young children starting from the ages of two through ten years of age.

Time out is extremely helpful in calming a situation that has gotten out of control. Many young children do not understand how to deal with their frustrations. From an early age, some children have a hard time learning how to stop the train before it hits the brick wall. By this I mean the child simply cannot calm himself when frustrated before he takes an impulsive, unacceptable action.

Heather wants to go next door to play, but you explain that she cannot go because dinner will be ready in a few minutes. She becomes sassy and disrespectful before throwing her Barbie dolls across the kitchen.

Arguing with Heather is not an option. She has been told no, you can't go, and the conversation is over. A time out is necessary to help Heather calm herself and understand that no means no.

According to *Time-out for Children* author Barbara Albers Hill,

This technique leaves the child's self-esteem intact in a way that no other form of discipline can. Simply and matter-of-factly, behavior problems are dealt with at the moment they occur, and this prevents the situation—and adult frustration—from escalating. Most important, a few minutes in isolation enable the child to:

- Reestablish self-control

- Clearly understand which behavior needs to change.

- See a cause-and-effect relationship between his misdeed and its result.

- Extinguish the target behavior through repetition and practice.

- Remain secure in his loving relation with the adult in charge.

- Earn immediate forgiveness.

Time out works because it extinguishes undesirable behavior in a way that leaves the child feeling renewed and responsible for his actions.

Now, *where* you send Heather for time out will make a world of difference.

I have tried using the corner, but that allowed my children to still interact with me. When children are in time out, they need to be removed from you completely. Not just for them to collect themselves, but for you to calm yourself as well. Children are not the only ones who suffer from frustration. Parents can be easily overwhelmed as well.

For children ages two and three years, I suggest using a playpen area in another room where they are safe. Always peek in every minute or so.

From the ages between four and six years, children begin to use the process of reasoning more skillfully. They can now sit on a chair in your bedroom or on the end of your bed for their time out.

A general rule is that the child should be in isolation for one minute for each year of their age.

Time out should not be comfortable, inviting, or stimulating. This area should be an isolated, reflective space. Translation: time out should be boring.

I struggled with where the time-out area should be once my children reached the age of seven. By then my bed was too comfortable to sit on, and they would happily go to time out. This consequence for undesirable behavior was no longer effective. So I had to think of a new place.

Then it came to me. The bathroom! You can't sneak an action figure out of the toy box, and it isn't quite as comfy and stimulating. Well… only sometimes. Potty breaks, as I refer to them, are quite a deterrent.

However, due to the potty-training process, it is important not to use the bathroom area as a time out until the child is completely toilet trained.

Now that we've discussed the time limits and suggested places for time out, it's important to stress explaining this new area to your child before you plan to enforce it. Don't wait until your child is in the throes of a tantrum to hear about Mom's new rule.

Next, ask yourself, *What am I striving for?* For one mother, good listening may be top priority because she has to tell Rusty to pick up his stuffed animals fifteen times before he even acknowledges the request.

For others, it may be sibling rivalry and safety issues. Being argumentative or disrespectful may be another good reason to use reflection of this kind. Whatever you are trying to teach your child, make sure they understand your expectations in advance.

Once you've confirmed your expectations, then it is time to act upon them. It is of the utmost importance that you follow through with the consequences once they have been established. No second chances and no negotiating.

To assure success, make sure the children understand that time out is a way of calming themselves down before getting hurt or making choices that will have a negative impact on them. Explain that it's also a time to think of ways to handle situations differently. Suggest counting to ten while frustrated.

Finally, some parents may ask, "How do you make a child stop arguing with you and get them in time out?" I like to call it: *Make your own luck.* My time out may only last seven minutes, depending on the age of the child, of course. But for each additional time I have to tell them to go to time out, they have earn an additional amount of minutes.

If one of my children finds himself in time out for fifteen minutes, I tell them I am sorry, but they made the choice to argue with me because my time out was only originally seven minutes. The children themselves earned unnecessary, additional minutes. This puts the responsibility completely on the child. Again, they learn that arguing is not tolerated and consequences are non-negotiable.

SHORT 'N SIMPLE

Debating with a child of any age is futile. It only serves to frustrate everyone. In order to reassure a child that they are safe and well taken care of, we must provide a shield of confidence.

By arguing with your child, you allow them to doubt your rules and abilities. Negotiating allows them to believe that you are second guessing your decisions.

If moms and dads are fair about their rules and the children understand what is expected, parents will have more credibility when things have calmed down. Communicate afterward how things could have been handled differently with better results.

No one wants an endless debate, that is, except the teenager that you just grounded for making an F on his report card. The reasons are endless why that F was not his fault. Apparently "the teacher doesn't like me," and "she didn't add my scores correctly," or, finally, "it doesn't look like an F to me!"

To debate such issues is a waste of time. What's more important is, did your teenager know that he would be grounded for an F on his report card? If so, the conversation is over. If not, you need to communicate your expectations more clearly.

Reasoning through your consequences during the punishment phase will only set you up for future failure. Let's say you have told eight-year-old Amanda that she wouldn't be able to watch TV in the afternoon if she forgot to make her bed in the morning.

The next morning she forgets to make her bed. When she comes home from school that afternoon, she begins to argue with you relentlessly until you give you one more chance. By negotiating you've taught Amanda that she doesn't have to suffer the consequence or make her bed if she wears you down by arguing.

When Amanda arrived home from school that afternoon, she should have been told, "Amanda, I'm afraid you forgot to make your bed this morning. No TV today. Period." If she begins arguing with you, she may need to have a potty break to understand arguing will not be tolerated, and a rule is a rule.

By keeping it short 'n simple, you remain calm and in control while keeping out of a useless debate. If you have already expressed your expectations, there is no reason to have to explain it over and over again.

THE TAKE-AWAY BLUES

Losing privileges is also an effective way of dealing directly with the problem swiftly. If you have told six-year-old Johnny not to throw the ball in the house and he has disobeyed you, Johnny should lose the privilege of playing with the ball. The child learns the direct logic between cause and effect.

The loss of one's privilege should be communicated beforehand so that there is no misunderstanding of your expectations. If you have never told Johnny not to throw the ball in the house, he has no idea he is breaking a rule.

If Kellie has been told not to roller blade without a helmet and she rides off into the wild blue yonder without a helmet, Kellie should lose the privilege of playing with her roller blades.

Taking away a privilege can be one of parents' most valuable learning tools because it has an immediate consequence related to the infraction.

When talking about issues that are in the gray area, such as dishonesty, it becomes a different ballgame as to what to take away. Your goal is not to make the child miserable but to teach them that lying is serious.

Parents should ask themselves, *What punishment would have an impact on him enough to think first before being dishonest in the future?*

To take away a child's time is also a loss of privilege. Most kids refer to this as being grounded. It can be more effective, however, if you have a positive attachment to it.

Telling a child to sit in his room all afternoon because he didn't tell the truth may make him miserable, but where is the lesson directly related to his lying? Remember, in our discipline strategy, a mom and dad's main objective is to teach.

I have several methods I use for this. Sometimes I will have them write the definition of truthfulness or honesty a number of times since they seem to be having a problem understanding their meanings.

If they have been insensitive to a sibling, maybe they need to write a list of twenty-five nice things about Alex.

Disrespectfulness may warrant being grounded to your room to write an essay on how important it is for each member of our family to respect one another as well as in our society.

One night our family went out to dinner with my husband's aunt and uncle who were visiting. Throughout the meal, I had to remind the boys to *stop* and keep their hands to themselves. They were not listening very well, and I, as all moms and dads feel from time to time, was embarrassed by their behavior. When we got into the car to leave the restaurant, I told them, "I was not very happy about your behavior tonight, boys. When we get home I want each of you to get a dictionary and write the definition of *stop* twenty-five times since you seem to have a problem with its meaning."

My eight-year-old, Josh, smiled slyly and said, "Sure, Mom, no problem. The definition of *stop* is 'halt.'" We all had a good chuckle. Then I made it a little clearer that I meant *my* definition in the dictionary!

Even small children who are learning to write their letters can practice writing the word *love* five times when they can't seem to display any for their younger sibling.

Older children can look up ten different words in a thesaurus for the word *civilized.*

I have found this to be a wonderful tool. By removing them to their rooms, they can concentrate on the lesson I have provided. No distractions.

Generally speaking, I tell the children they may come out of their rooms when their sentences or lessons are complete. In this way, the children control how much time they will be grounded to their rooms. This disciplinary method helps with letter-writing skills for small children, dictionary skills for elementary children and essay writing skills for older children. I have found that when you give a child the chance to write sentences or essays about how to be kind to a sibling or even to write the definition of kindness, it serves as a *positive mantra* and actually reinforces the better behavior. To have them write about anything negative such as dishonesty is a wasted use of energy. I encourage children to think of ways to be more kind, more honest, more respectful.

The bottom line is that by using their own words and thoughts, this method incorporates positive messages into a personal core belief system that teaches the children character, integrity, respect for others as well as how to react more appropriately in future situations.

Most important of all: It works!

STICK YOUR TONGUE OUT!

As moms and dads, we are constantly in a position of playing judge and jury. Did Susie kick Danny, or did Danny kick Susie? Did Chris track in mud all over the floor, or was it Larry? And who flicked pudding all over the ceiling?

It's a tough job being a parent. We're constantly expected to know the truth at all times.

I would love to claim this technique as my own, but it was used by my mother and works beautifully on small children.

The basic premise of this system is simple. When four-year-old Ryan tells you he did not hide his brother's school shoes, there is only one way to get at the truth. Ryan needs to stick out his tongue.

After telling the child that a parent can tell if they are lying by their tongues, have them stick out their tongues. Nine times out of ten, if a child is lying, they will only stick their tongues out part of the way. If they want you to know they are innocent, they will say, "Ahh!"

This is not deceitful because the parent *can* tell if a child is lying by their tongues! It works like a charm, and my husband and I have gotten more than enough belly laughs (in private!) from this method. It really works!

TO SPANK OR NOT TO SPANK— THAT IS THE QUESTION

Whew! Physical punishment is one controversial subject! It comes down to only this: self-control. If parents do not have self-control, they have no business using spanking as a form of discipline.

However, in some instances, it can be useful if used as an instrument that is saved for issues of safety and extreme cases of defiance and disrespect.

By my definition, a spanking is a swift pop on the bottom to get the attention of the child. This type of discipline is used to swiftly reinforce your expectations. When an undesirable behavior is serious enough, a parent should be prepared to take action. Spankings should be used for children approximately eighteen months to ten years old.

Again I quote Dr. James Dobson on this issue:

> Many children desperately need this resolution to their disobedience. In those situations when the child fully understands what he is being asked to do or not to do but refuses to yield to adult leadership, an appropriate spanking is the shortest and most effective route to an attitude adjustment.

Some parents may feel that children will become violent if spanked. Yes, it is true that if children are subjected to violent beatings, slapping, or other unjust physical punishments, they could develop a violent nature.

However, my definition of spanking and violent beatings are worlds apart.

Dr. Dobson goes on to say,

> When a parent administers a reasonable spanking in response to willful disobedience, a nonverbal message is being given to the child. He must understand that there are not only dangers in the physical world to be avoided. He should also be wary of dangers in his social world, such as defiance, sassiness, selfishness, temper tantrums, behavior that puts his life in danger, etc. The minor pain that is associated with this deliberate misbehavior tends to inhibit it, just as discomfort works to shape behavior in the physical world.

When three-year-old Kevin runs out into the street while you're screaming no, he may get a pop on the bottom to get his direct attention. Kevin needs to understand that going in the street is dangerous and will result in an immediate and firm consequence. In this instance, spanking is a useful and swift punishment.

When in a public area, always try to take your children to a private area to discipline them, whether verbally reprimanding them or popping them on the bottom. There is always a bathroom or a hallway that you can slide into in order to get his/her attention without making a spectacle out of them or you.

As with any discipline technique, spanking is a personal choice. If spanking your child is not right for you, find another form of discipline. There are plenty to choose from! If you have chosen to spank, then keep in mind that spanking should only be used to get their attention for more serious issues. Physical punishment should not be an intimidation device. Spanking should establish your control, not exhibit your lack of it. It is a tool to teach the children that certain behaviors are harmful or simply will not be tolerated... never to hurt the child.

UNITED WE STAND; DIVIDED WE FALL

This section deals with the subject of parental support for one another. The mom and dad that present a united front will have a much higher success rate in their endeavors.

But as with any area of raising children, there are gray areas. There will be times that your husband does not agree with your decision to ground your daughter. He may feel your decision was too harsh for her behavior. You may feel that your husband should not have told your son he could not go to a friend's house.

In raising children, moms and dads will make mistakes but should disagree as loving, involved parents. A child needs to know that parents are united together as a team despite these disagreements.

I suggest being honest with your child. "Mandy, this is something your father and I will discuss privately. We will get back to you with our decision." This doesn't mean, "Mandy, I'll see if I can get Daddy to change his mind so you can go to the party."

Two-year-old Katie wants a chocolate chip cookie. "No, Katie, no cookie." You offer her a banana. She rejects your offer by throwing herself on the floor, screaming. If Daddy walks into the kitchen, reaches for the cookie, and hands it to Katie, what mixed signal has Daddy given Katie? Katie just learned that "No, Katie" really doesn't mean no at all.

The mom and dad are upper management of your family business and this partnership does not include the children. A clear understanding of this will save parents a tremendous amount of manipulation and heartache in the future.

So what do we do when one of the leaders of the family business forgets his/her commitment to teamwork and plays good cop/bad cop after an agreed-upon rule has been violated? Well… for starters, there's always *the look*. We've all been there and seen that! If that look had laser capabilities, none of us would have to worry about a second fall from grace, that's for sure!

But on a serious note, that's where the great divide should end. A quiet discussion in the back room to get back on track is all that is necessary in situations such as these when one member of the team falls off the horse. As busy, on-the-go parents, we all get tired. We all give in sometimes just for the sake of a little peace and quiet. That's the reality of it. As I've stated before, this book is not to help you create perfect scenarios in your household. There will never be any such thing. The important thing is to get back on the horse and continue as a team. Everyone has a weak moment now and then. There's no sense in making a mountain out of a mole hill for the sake of one forbidden cookie!

LOVE MEANS SAYING YOU'RE SORRY

In the movie *Love Story*, Ali McGraw softly replies to Ryan O'Neal, "Love means never having to say you're sorry." I hated that line. Of course you need to say you're sorry, especially to the ones you love!

As mothers and fathers, as hard as wel try, we can't be right all the time. Perhaps this is the most relieving lessons of all. We will never be the perfect parent, nor will our children be the perfect child.

When you have made a mistake, apologize to your child. Let them know that you have taken the time and given the situation a great deal of consideration. If she is right, let her know she is right. Explain to her that being a parent is difficult sometimes, and while we try to do the right things, sometimes we make mistakes too.

By allowing our children to see our human side, we teach them to be free to apologize when they have failed us as well. Acknowledging your failures is the beginning of a relationship of mutual respect between moms and dads and children.

It's a tough job for parents to balance their expectations, priorities, and consequences equally with unconditional love and open communication. Being exclusively a fun parent will not bring the happiness and stability to your child's life.

All children need balance. Where there is balance, there is harmony. Where balance is absent, there is chaos. This balance should be made up of self-discipline, expectations, a zest for living, creativity, and always with a sense of humor.

A Package Deal: The Blended Family

Jeannette was on her way home from the office when her cell phone rang. "Hello?" she answered politely.

"It's me honey," Jack said happily. "I just wanted to let you know Heidi was here. I told her all about you, and she was really excited to be meeting you tonight."

The beating of Jeannette's heart was so robust; she could actually hear it in her head. *Do I really want to meet his daughter? What if she is this horrible brat that spray paints cats blue for Daddy's attention? What if he expects me to baby sit?*

Driving into the driveway of Jack's home, Jeanette got her first glimpse of Heidi. She looked small for six years old. Her tousled blonde hair had a ring from what used to be a ponytail. The rubber band was now sagging, holding only the lucky ends together. Heidi stopped roller skating on the sidewalk when she saw Jeannette's car pull up.

Nervously, Jack rose from the front porch swing and led Heidi to Jeannette. "Heidi, honey, this is my new friend, the lady I was telling you about last night. Her name is Jeannette. Can you say hello, darling?"

Heidi squinted her crystal-blue eyes almost shut to block out the sun and sized up her daddy's new friend. In the moments of silence that followed, Jeannette's heart was pounding deafeningly loud. "I-I brought you a little something, Heidi. I hope you like it," she stammered to the child.

Heidi grabbed the new Barbie doll out of Jeannette's hand and ran to the front door. Jack seemed horrified. Before he could begin making apologies, Heidi turned and made her way back to where Jeannette and Jack were standing, dumbfounded, in the driveway.

"By the way, lady, you have a moustache. My daddy doesn't like ladies that have moustaches."

Note to self: hide the cat!

The alarmingly high rate of divorce in this country is no secret and it even appears at times that we have become desensitized toward it. Our neighborhoods are filled with the heartbreak of broken families and the determination of others to start over in order to form new *blended* families. As women's rights took hold in the 1960s, and our endless opportunities opened up, divorce rates went up just as quickly. It was no longer necessary for couples to stay in a loveless or abusive relationship. Everyone has the right to personal happiness. Vow or no vow.

Divorce is an extremely painful time for any man or woman. The dissolution of a marriage is truly a death. The death of what two people had hoped for but had been unable to achieve together.

There is no shame in admitting this mistake. We are all human, with human frailties. Some couples truly love one another but simply cannot live together. Some couples have past issues that sabotage the relationship. Some people simply feel unlovable. Some people *are* unlovable.

Divorce is not the end to one's life. Divorce should be the beginning of a commitment to a better way of living.

That said, it is important for anyone involved in a relationship with a partner who is divorced to be respectful and nurturing. No one plans to be divorced. Even if the choice to divorce may have been their own, this unexpected detour can be equally as shattering as it is for the spouse who never wanted the divorce at all. This scenario is tragic enough with two people floundering around, trying to pick up the pieces of their lives, trying to move on. Add the new insecurities of the children to this emotional tsunami and we begin to understand how any new step parent being added to the mix has the potential for being a recipe for disaster.

But it doesn't have to be. A beautiful new family can be born from the ashes. And you may be the one person in the world who can make it all come together.

It's essential for anyone in a relationship with children from a previous marriage to fully understand it's *a package deal.* Whether you are bringing children into the marriage or step-parenting your husband's children, the commitment to form a blended family unit must be solidified with both partners. Blended families can be such a blessing. With a little love and attention, most seeds will blossom into something spectacular.

GOOD DAD, GOOD MATE!

Most likely when you began dating your husband, some of the things you loved most about him were his compassion, his affection, his devotion, and his loyalty. (If he's handsome too, then you most certainly got yourself a catch!) These are golden qualities that are necessary for any loving relationship.

Time is a good indicator of someone's ability to go the distance. Some partners are intrigued by the newness of a relationship, but their dedication slowly fades. Others are stayers and will love you even when they see you in the morning before your coffee.

Raising any child is an endurance test. (Amen to that!)

How he parents is a real test of what kind of man he is. Any man who denies his child will more than likely eventually deny you. A man who forgets his child's birthday will more than likely forget yours too. A man who rarely communicates with his child will most likely not want a personal relationship with you also.

It's also important to note that if a man emotionally abandons his child from a previous marriage, he will more than likely emotionally abandon a child with you.

Before you choose to marry a man with children from a previous marriage, you need to ask yourself the following questions:

1. Is he affectionate and loving with his child?

2. Is he committed to calling his child and spending quality time with his child?

3. Is he trying to slowly incorporate me into their lives?

4. Does he remember special events in his child's life that are important to the child?

5. Is he willing to make personal sacrifices for his child?

If you are able to answer yes to three or more of these questions, you have found yourself a good man! If not, talk with your husband about your feelings toward his relationship with his child. But know this: Taking on the role of a stepparent does not mean you have to take over your husbands' inefficiencies. A stepparent's participation should be considered an extra… extra love, extra support, an extra set of arms for hugs.

Your husband may need your loving guidance to show him how to relate to his or your child. Some men are often intimidated with the role of parenting. Some feel ill equipped and insecure. By talking about your husband's issues, you may be able to help him have a better relationship with his child.

It may be awkward in the beginning as you embark on your new role as step mother to your husband's children. It will be difficult to know the parameters with how to balance the needs of everyone involved in your new blended family.

Questions may arise:

1. Do I discipline his children the same as I do our own children?
    Answer: Yes. Exactly the same, with the same fairness and objectives in mind. But as with your biological children, explain the rules of your home first so there are no misunderstandings.

2. Do I give them chores around the house just as the other children have chores and responsibilities?
    Answer: Yes. Even visiting step children will need to do chores. Otherwise they will always feel like merely guests in your home and not actual family members.

3. Will I ever learn to love these children as I do my own?
    Answer: Yes. You will if you open your heart wide enough to let them in. They need you. Regardless of how their actions may dictate otherwise, they need your love. And you are the woman for the job.

All children, whether stepchildren or biological children, need the attention and involvement from both parents. If there are family issues from either side concerning the roles within the family unit, I strongly urge you to seek professional counseling.

Each member of your family depends on the harmony of your family to be happy and successful. If you are experiencing problems that are out of your control, a third party can be extremely beneficial.

The reality is a marriage involving stepchildren can be rocky sometimes. However, if both partners are dedicated, loving, and supportive of each other, your family can thrive well beyond your expectations.

The following are some thoughts to consider when committing to a package deal.

THE OTHER WOMAN

When you become a stepmother, realize one thing: you are officially the other woman. I don't care how wonderful you are as a stepmother or how hard you try in the beginning; both you and your stepchild will more than likely feel like you are in competition for the same man's heart.

When I first met Kellie Jean, she was the longest, lankiest nine-year-old I had ever seen. She had thick, dark-brown hair and inquisitive hazel eyes.

Kellie was not quite sure of me in the beginning. (Maybe it was my moustache.) Maybe it's because she was from a home where both parents had chosen the wrong partners, twice.

Kellie's mother and Frank had married at a very young age and divorced when she was three years old. She had no real understanding of family when I met her.

Kellie had a good relationship with her own mother and let me know from the beginning that she did not need another mother. Before I ever said, "I do," to Frank, I had already become *the other woman* to Kellie. The other woman who she worried would try to replace her biological mother and the other woman who was competing for her daddy's love. Double jeopardy.

I did not resent my position in her life. I liked to think of my role in raising Kellie as someone extra. I would never dream of trying to compete with her mother, although at the time, I imagine, this is most certainly how she must have felt. Over the years our relationship has blossomed into a loving friendship, which I attribute a lot to Kellie's patience with me and my desire to make her understand that she was a part of our family whether she lived with us or not.

Regardless of what the situation was concerning Kellie, and she wasn't always a happy camper with our decisions, I felt she always knew we loved her and had her best interests at heart. Kellie's place in our family was unconditional.

Today, Frank, Kellie's mother, and I are so proud to say that Kellie has risen to the rank of Staff Sergeant with the United States Marine Corp, with two beautiful babies of her own. She is a wonderful mother and a lovely young woman. Family is very important to her, and I'd like to think that having two loving families to raise her helped make her the success she is today.

Love works in mysterious ways. The anxiety I felt over becoming the stepmother to someone else's child and living through some rough times with Kellie luckily did not deter me from diving in with both feet. I have learned so much from being in Kellie's life and take such pride in knowing that maybe, just maybe, she learned a little about life from me too.

Eight-year-old Jason adores his daddy. To Jason, his daddy's new wife Emily, is merely the lady who makes his daddy's dinner and washes his clothes. It is difficult for him to understand that Daddy could possibly love anyone else beside him and his mom. Jason often wonders if his daddy will stop loving him like he did his mother. He really wants to ask his real mom if a dad can divorce his own son too, but he's too afraid to because she still cries at the kitchen table late at night. Her sadness makes Jason dislike Daddy's new wife. A lot.

Sometimes to understand the behavior of others we have to put ourselves in their shoes. As the stepparent, you are the adult in the situation. You are responsible for understanding the insecurities and needs of the child even if the child's behavior is negative toward you.

Children cannot comprehend what goes on in our adult world. They are afraid of your marriage to their daddy because the last one brought so much unrest and tears. Why should little Dawn trust you? You replaced her mother!

When parents of children remarry, it is, in a way, a betrayal. Dawn's father is expecting her to be nice to the other woman in his life. He is expecting his child to trust you as her new mother. However, the trust for the step parent can take years to achieve. So be prepared to be patient. The road to a loving relationship can be long and very trying. But staying the course can result in one of the most rewarding relationships you will ever have.

As you begin your quest to combine families into one loving unit, some children can become angry, confused, and belligerent. It is the child's way of taking her daddy's attention away from you and establishing that she is still number one in his life by controlling his attention with negative behavior.

A stepmother in this situation needs to be understanding and patient. Consistent love, calmness, and tolerance will show the child that you are willing to go the distance with your new family.

The following are some ideas to help you bond with your stepchild:

The first step toward being a successful step-mother is sitting down and talking with your stepchild.

1. Tell the child that you are not replacing their mother. Explain that you understand how much they love their mother and you would never try to replace that relationship.

2. Tell the child how happy you are to see how much she and her daddy love each other. Explain that a father's love and a husband's love for his wife are two different kinds of love.

3. Ask the child to tell you some funny stories about when they were little while their mom and dad were still married. This is difficult to do, I know, but it allows the child to see that you are not trying to deny or erase the past.

4. When appropriate, hug them a lot.

BIOLOGICAL MOMS

Now it is important that we turn our attention to the biological mother in this scenario. Your husband has remarried, giving your child a new stepmom. This event can spawn fresh, raw feelings.

As the biological mother, you may feel ecstatic that your ex-husband found someone so lovely to be in your child's life. Lucky you!

However, you may feel wounded and jealous and rejected. It can at times even physically hurt you inside when your daughter Jane comes home from visiting Dad and goes on and on about how much fun she had with her new stepmom, Sarah.

You may feel superior to his new wife. Nothing Sarah does is the way you do things for Johnny.

You may feel vindictive. If you can't be happy, why should your ex-husband be happy?

All of these feelings can be overwhelming to the biological mother. Whether you have remarried or not, you still feel protective and want to be in full control of your children. It is a natural instinct within all mothers. To share this control with another mother is not an easy task. But it is the most self-sacrificing thing you can do for the good of your child during this complicated transition.

Your child/children will be taking their cues from you. They will study how you interact with their father, and they will listen to how you speak to their new stepmother. If all parties involved are calm and respectful, the transition for your child/children will be much easier. If all parties involved create an impossible impasse with each and every decision made concerning the children, the cue will be for the children to react with adverse negativity as well.

The key word in this situation is *control*.

You are Johnny's mother. No one can take that title away from you, and Johnny will always love you as his mother. But here is the reality of your post-divorce plight. If you choose to barricade yourself by clinging on to old wounds and being difficult in order to get back at his father, you are only going to hurt Johnny.

All children from divorce go through various degrees of struggle. This new transition for Johnny is not going to be an easy road. Every time he spends the weekend with his dad and his step mother, more than likely he is going to feel as though he is betraying you, especially if you are angry and upset when he leaves your home. There are no winners in this predicament.

If control is what you seek, then take control of yourself and choose to make it work with Johnny's new family. There is no greater gift you can give to him at this moment in his life that will impact him more. Johnny needs his father in his life. Help him to feel good about going to spend time with his dad's new family. Listen graciously to his stories from the weekend that includes his new step mother. If there are any issues you have with what is going on, call your ex-husband privately. The children do not need the added stress of listening to two adults bicker over eating candy for breakfast at Dad's house. Pick your battles carefully. A peaceful co-existence with both families is truly in the best interest of your child. It takes a great deal of courage and forgiveness to let go of a painful past. But do it for Johnny.

Remember, you and your husband were not the only casualties that resulted from your divorce. Johnny needs to have calm and mature adults willing to do what's best for him. Help Johnny understand that it's okay for him to learn to love his new step mother too.

Children have enough love within to go around for everyone. Try not to worry and have faith. You will not be forgotten.

You will always be Johnny's mom. First. Last. Always. (So don't be a fruitcake!)

Here are some positive steps that you can incorporate into your home to create a happy balance with your blended family:

Keep Mum about the Other Mom

Don't get caught in this trap. As your relationship grows with your children and stepchildren, they will often confide in you, concerning issues with their other biological mother. This is a wonderful stride in your relationship with your stepchildren, and you should be proud of yourself that the children feel trust enough to complain about their mothers.

However, your job is to listen. In fact, when reasonable, try to explain to the child the mother's position and why she might be reacting that way. A good way to be neutral is to begin with, "Well, I can understand why you might feel that way, but perhaps your mom was looking at it this way... " Keeping it neutral in this way shows Jessica that you can't be persuaded into jumping on the *biological-mom-bashing band wagon* quite so easily. Regardless of the awful things Jessica says about her mother, which may or may not be true, trust me, she does not want you to agree with her. And more than this, you do not want anything disrespectful you've said to jeopardize the good relationship you've worked hard to achieve with her mother.

A quick story: One morning, when my boys were young, their wise, old pre-school teacher told me, "I'll make a deal with you. I'll believe only half of what the boys say about you if you promise to only believe half of what they say about me."

Emotions run high in dramatic, hormonal teenagers. You'll need to develop a keen ear for most stories to decipher what you truly need to react to and what you just need to listen to and shake off as teenage angst. But just as it is important for the biological mother to support your relationship with Jessica as her step mother, you will need to support her as well.

All parties deserve and need the benefit of the doubt.

In addition to *telling on* the other parent, some children will try to play one parent against the other. By staying neutral, you are also setting the boundaries around the triangle of power. The child should always be the center of this triangle. By respecting this position, all parents involved can avoid the risk of undermining the decisions of the other parent.

In so many families, there can be animosity between the old wife and the new wife. The other wife may choose to say unflattering things about you. She may create chaos, even fabricate stories to show you in an unfavorable light.

Stay above anything like this. Remind yourself you are a gracious lady. Take the high road and steer your behavior with the voice of reason. Not only will you be showing that you're above it all, but you will be setting a calm example for the children as well as their biological mother.

A simple response to defend yourself is all that is needed when a negative verbal attack occurs:

"I'm sorry, but I would never have said or done that."

End of discussion.

Some good rules to follow when dealing with the other mother are:

- Be kind and courteous.

- Stay out of business that doesn't directly affect you.

- Show her that you have a genuine interest in the well being of the children.

All mothers are protective of their young. If you give her no reason to doubt your love for the children and you're honest and kind hearted, she hardly has any ammunition against you. Thus a harmonious extended family. What more could you ask for? (I know, I know, an ex-wife that's *not* a fruitcake!)

Initiate Daddy's Night with the Child
By establishing some time alone with their daddy, you are showing your understanding for how things used to be.

Make reservations for your husband to take your stepdaughter to dinner and a play or a ballgame for your stepson. These small tokens of respect will go a long way in slowly earning the trust of your stepchildren.

When you plan a daddy's night out, you are not separating your family. On the contrary, you are showing the ultimate love for your family. It takes a gracious lady to step aside and allow her new family to unfold naturally. You are that gracious lady. Give the children time and space to grow to love you slowly by respecting their need for private time with Daddy.

Don't Try to Win the Children's Love by Buying Their Affections

Big mistake. Children can see straight through this one. Will they try to get you to do a little guilt spending? Will they affectionately tell you how much better they like you than their own mother, especially if you bought that new pair of shoes? Absolutely.

Again, don't get stuck in this quicksand. You will never be able to crawl out from this never-ending game of *I'll like you if you buy me ...*

You are the adult. Allow the children to understand that the greatest gift you can give to them is not bought with money. It is a sense of family and all that goes with it. Family dinners, movie nights, slumber parties, as well as Saturday family workdays, and cleaning the kitchen together.

I used to tell Kellie that if I gave her everything she wanted, then I would be robbing her of the thrill of waiting for something special. Was she thrilled with that? No way. In fact, I think she probably huffed off to her room, mumbling something about me being a wicked stepmother. (It's not always fun, folks!)

But I took a vow to love Kellie to the best of my ability and raise her like my own. I do not give my own children everything they want because it is not in their best interest. Giving into Kellie Jean would, I believe, send a message that I didn't care enough to take the time to discipline her the same way I did the boys.

We talked earlier about delayed gratification, and no child is an exception to this rule. They deserve to *not* be spoiled too. Giving in to a stepchild and having separate rules for the biological children only makes them feel more isolated from the family. They rationalize, "If I'm treated differently, then I must be different."

Of course, the children are going to roll their eyes at you and give you a *whatever*, but deep down inside, even though they really wanted those shoes, they are glad that you didn't give in. Parents that say no are ironically reassuring to their children. Stepchildren are no different.

GOING TO DAD'S: VACATION CITY!

For children that reside the majority of time with the other parent, they are constantly torn by the guilt of not being with the other parent. Think about it: at such an early age, they have had to share two completely different lives.

Mom may be very strict and demanding. She may have expectations like making their beds, making good grades, and cleaning the kitchen.

Going to Dad's, however, may be a totally different story! *It's vacation time!* Usually every other weekend and summers, they get to stay up late and eat popcorn for dinner. Who cares about the dishes? Total euphoria!

Again, another mistake. This is not only confusing to the child and not fair to the biological mother, but most especially it is unfair to any step parent to have to put on Disney on Parade every time the child comes to visit!

A good idea is to have a family meeting with all parents to determine what the rules are going to be. If bedtime is eight p.m., then bedtime is eight p.m. at both households. If chores are expected at one household, then chores should be initiated at the secondary household.

This type of double teaming the children is a wonderful way to show them that everyone involved has their best interest in mind. It helps your relationship with the ex-wife because she feels her wishes are respected in regards to raising the children.

Also, you're not exhausted from entertaining all weekend, and their mother or father is not furious that their homework didn't get done. All sides win.

MY FAIR LADY

Be fair. The rules in your family should apply to all members of your family. If your rule is that everyone wears a helmet while skateboarding, all children should wear a helmet, whether you are a stepchild or not. All children should be treated equally within the family unit.

Your stepchildren should be included in family vacations, family photos when possible, Christmas, and other meaningful holidays.

It's important for all children to know they are missed and loved when they are not present for family functions. On the occasions that Kellie could not be with us, we would send cards to say we missed her for Halloween, Easter, etc.

There should be no guilty messages attached for choosing to spend the holiday with their other parent. That's a tough spot for any child to be in. Remind them to have fun and that you can't wait to see them again soon.

By creating an environment that's fair, you are allowing your family to gel together, disregarding any differences between the children. This is a foundation that any family can and will flourish in.

There is no doubt that being a stepmother to a child from a divorced home can be rough. There will be days you don't want the job. There will be days you won't be qualified for the job. There will be days you will want to tell your husband where he *and* his child can go ... (Not your best moment). But what if you were the one person in the world that child needed in his life to become a successful adult? What if by giving up on the child, you robbed him of the opportunity of really understanding the beauty and the comfort of belonging to a loving family? What if by standing your ground and loving an unlovable child, you were able to break through and become one of the greatest influences in his life?

All children deserve a chance. In fact, it is the most frustrating, unlovable children that need us most. By never giving up on a child, you teach them that family is binding, unconditional, and a foundation of security that will long outlast our lives.

Whenever you are ready to throw in the towel, remind yourself that if this unruly child were your biological child, you could only hope that your husband would be patient enough to love him the way you do.

Love can mend animosity, love can heal wounds, and love can make even the most broken of hearts love again. The child of divorce is broken hearted. Your love can help in the mending of their fragile little souls.

Last but not least, these children are an extension of your marriage. This man came to you as a package deal, and vice versa. This package deal can be a blessing or a disaster. Unfortunately a lot of the success of the family depends on how you handle everyone involved.

Luckily, most women are naturally nurturing, loving, kind, and gracious. We are able to take unpleasant situations and make them workable with a hug and a smile. It is our gift. Don't waste your talents judging a child who is incapable of expressing themselves any other way than how they are feeling at the moment. *Show* the child how to love by loving them first. The rest will follow.

In closing this chapter, I will not lie to you: making a blended family work is not easy. It takes perseverance, compassion, love, patience, and sometimes a great therapist! But nothing in life that's easy is ever quite as rewarding as overcoming the obstacle you never dreamed you could scale over. I can only urge you to stay the course and try your best to bring everyone in your family together. You *are* the woman for the job. (Unless, of course, you are the fruitcake).

By the way, I haven't referred to myself, with the exception of this book for practical purposes, as Kellie's *stepmom* for many years. She is my daughter. And I am proud to say, I am her mother. Too.

Your Husband, Low Man on the Totem Pole: Caring for Your Man

Close your eyes and imagine being your husband in this scenario:

The children are playing joyfully on a freshly cut lawn in the backyard. There is no screaming or fighting, just laughter. (Just go with me on this one; it's hypothetical!)

The Major League Baseball Playoffs are on the tube, and the remote control is warm from resting in your hand all afternoon. A woman enters the room. She's beautiful. Stan thinks to himself, *What a smart guy I was to have married her.*

This vision of loveliness brings him another beer and bends over his favorite brown plaid recliner and whispers, "I want you... now." Stan points to the TV, shrugs his shoulders, and implies that he'd love to, but the game is still on. She smiles and saunters into the kitchen to make him a sandwich instead. Stan promises her he'll take care of her... later. She giggles at how funny he is.

What a shame Stan has to wake up from this promising dream. I'm sure it is lovely while it lasted, but reality? Sorry, Stan. Few of our men get this lucky. A baseball game on a Saturday afternoon? I don't think so! Erica's bicycle tires need to be patched, the shrubs need to be topped off, and the garage has so many webs in it that the spiders are spinning *clean me* messages from every corner.

With the arrival of children, "I want you... now" becomes "*I want you now!*" Same words, totally different implications. And make you a sandwich? Maybe on my next break!

With so many responsibilities, our relationships with our spouses are lost in the shuffle. Between dance recitals, Boy Scout meetings, sleepovers, and little league baseball playoffs, where do husbands go?

When you began the dating phase of your relationship, your attention was directed at getting to know this interesting person sitting next to you.

You sat down for long conversations and coffee, laughed at each other's jokes, devoted evenings to listening to one another's day, and encouraged personal dreams. You complimented one another, dressed up for one another, called each other during your lunch break just to say, "I miss you."

In the evenings you'd put on a Billy Joel CD, turned the lights low, and kissed for hours.

When you both decided you couldn't live without the other another second here on earth, you pledged your love and devotion and bought rings to signify your undying commitment to each other.

After the wedding, things moved along great, though you didn't find it cute anymore that he left his underwear on the bathroom floor.

He looked at your toiletries on the bathroom counter and in his wildest dreams couldn't imagine how one person could need so many creams and lotions. But the under garments that draped over the shower had to go.

Slowly the relationship entered into a safe zone where you both were very comfortable. You still held hands at the movie and cooked pasta together. Every day you'd learn something new about the other.

As time goes by, you get married and settle in for the long haul. You both put on a couple of pounds, and his attention span for your latest spat with your girlfriend is between little and none, and you swear if he tells you the joke about the goat again you're going to clobber him.

But sex is still terrific, and there are times you both can't keep your hands off of each other. Your drive is somewhere between animal passion and complete loss of self when you are together.

You have your sexy secrets that you both giggle over. There's mood lighting, soft music, and lovemaking is slow and intimate. Nothing else matters but being together and in the moment.

Each day you thank God for each other and plan for your future together. Together, you make a wonderful team despite the little things that you both willingly overlook.

Then one day a home pregnancy test says positive. Scared and excited, you both plan to expand your family with the birth of a little one. A baby. What could be better for your relationship than the birth of a baby?

As the months go by, your belly begins to take on a life of its own. Your husband stares at you getting out of the shower. His look is a look that is both puzzled and frightened at the same time. Will it *ever* go away? And what's up with those extra-large panties?

In his own way, he tries to be complimentary: "Well, at least you're not as fat as Uncle Ernest!" He attempts to be funny and make you laugh. But he's not funny.

You cry for no reason and eat whatever is not nailed down. You chatter nonstop about cribs, which diapers to use, and which car seat is the best. He is interested but suggests you call your mom and ask her instead since he is not an authority on that kind of stuff. Besides, there's a Clint Eastwood marathon on television, and he'd really hate to miss *that!*

You cry again.

Finally the big day arrives, and your water breaks. Time to go to the hospital. Between hee-hee hoo-hoo, he asks if you'd like him to stop on the way and get you a hamburger. When you say, "No, hee-hee, thanks, hoo-hoo," he asks if you would mind if he zipped through and got himself something since you didn't have time to fix him breakfast that morning. Judging by your look, he smartly drives you to the hospital and forgets the hamburger.

Thirteen hours later, the doctor hands you a healthy, beautiful baby boy. You both count toes and stare in amazement that you created this incredible creature together. A family at last!

For some families, the birth of a baby is the beginning and an end all in the same cosmic moment. It's the beginning because you have just reproduced the very best of yourselves into a new spirit. This spirit will bring joy to your lives that no one could ever explain with words. Children are a gift beyond description. Hence the beginning of a life with a cherished baby.

But it is also an end. The ending of just the two of us. Now there is no such thing.

It's easy to see how couples can drift apart. Both moms and dads are on overdrive for the good of the family. Husbands are working extra hours to pay for insurance and diapers, and wives are overwhelmed with laundry and hungry babies around the clock.

Yet while every muscle in your body aches at the end of the day, it takes virtually no energy at all to be kind to your man. A simple "How was your day, honey?" before drifting off the sleep, or "You sure looked handsome in that new blue shirt today."

Men have tremendous egos. He needs to be told he is doing a great job at work and how proud you are of him. He needs to feel attractive and desirable as a man.

Having children opens up so many avenues for each couple. Here are a few of the roads you don't want to go down:

- The Ignore Your Man Highway

Your husband may not want a complete dissertation on your life, nor does he want to tell you his, but he wants to be noticed. If he walks in the door each day only to be handed a baby because you've had enough, resentment can creep in.

- The My Day was Harder Than Your Day Highway

Your daily struggles as a family should not be a contest. Try to steer away from starting this no-win deadlock.

- The I Have the Kids Eight to Five p.m.; It's Your Turn! Highway

Accept the fact that you are both wiped out and doing your share for the betterment of your family. He's working hard to support the family; you are working hard to raise the family. When marriages start to cruise down this highway, it's time for some serious time alone together to catch your breath.

Remind yourselves that having a family is a tremendous change, sometimes good and realistically sometimes not so good. You both took a vow to love one another and to be kind to each other. Kindness breeds kindness. Be gentle with each other, and nurture each other's tired spirits. Start talking again. Get to know him all over again. What makes him happy? What makes him feel attractive?

Men and women have different ideas of marriage and happiness. You might be surprised how different!

One of the first steps to rekindling the sparks of your relationship is accepting each other's differences. Of course, one of the biggest differences between husbands and wives (excluding communication) is sex.

1. How often is too much?

2. During foreplay, why do I wonder if the clothes in the dryer are done?

3. Do too many quickies mean we're not in love anymore?

4. And why does a twenty-minute nap mean more to me than ten minutes of passionate sex with my husband lately?

There are several reasons for these questions, but let's start with a few truths:

1. Men view sex differently than women.
    This is not to say one aspect is better or worse than the other, just different.

2. Most women need romance with their sex. We like the long, drawn-out version of sexual tension. We like long walks, holding hands, eternity-lasting sensual kissing, and extensive foreplay. Music in the background is a must, and candles are a wonderful touch. The children must be asleep, preferably when they have a minor cold and you have given them some sort of cough suppressant medication that assures they are asleep and won't

barge in the room unexpectedly. Men, the majority of the time, just need you. They don't need props, music, petting, foreplay, bantering, a complete explanation of your feelings, and they don't even need the lights out. (Weird.) That is not to say that romance is unimportant to men. It definitely is important. It's just not *as* important all of the time.

3. Accept that your ideas of sex are completely different. Sex is a time of giving, sharing, exploring, and learning about each other's desires and needs.

4. There's nothing wrong with a quickie!

    In fact, if that's all the energy you both have to give after working all day and taking care of the kids, go for it! Sex can be a great stress reliever as well, so don't think that sex has to be an all-consuming, passionate experience 100 percent of the time. Stay connected at all costs.

5. One of the biggest mistakes a woman/man can make when dealing with their sex lives is assuming the partner knows what they want.

    Girls, don't wait for your husband to know that you want candles. Get them out yourself and light up! By supposing that your husband knows you want hot oils and massaging, you are setting him up for a battle he can never win. Some men just don't have a romance mentality. But this does not mean they don't love it when you create this environment. When you love someone, you have the obligation to help him make you happy. By complaining that he should just know makes you an unhappy martyr.

Besides, while it may not occur to your husband to initiate music, candles, and slow dancing, he will most certainly enjoy the evening with you. And maybe, just maybe, he will enjoy it so much that he will follow your lead unexpectedly!

6. If your relationship is kind, supporting, nurturing, and affectionate during the day, this same gentleness can spill over into your bedroom.

If you have been Broom Hilda all day long, ranting about what a loser your husband is for breaking the lawn mower that afternoon, and he tells you at dinner he's had a steak that was burned less at a truck stop in Kansas, realistically, any kind of gentle sensuality has gone out the window for that evening.

However, when you are supportive, accepting, helpful, and loving during the day to one another, gentleness can creep back into your lives... In other words, bite your tongue and remember the golden rule (For those who don't remember the golden rule: If you don't have something kind to say, keep it to yourself... and call your sister and tell *her* what a thoughtless jerk he was that morning.)

7. Men love their wives just the way they are, extra baby pounds an' all! It's no secret that after childbirth, we don't look like Cindy Crawford any-

more, (did we ever?) but in most cases, our body shapes matter more to us than to our husbands.

8. The biggest player in the sex game is the brain. In most relationships, it really doesn't matter about your body size or shape at all. If you *feel* sexy, you will be sexy. It's all a mental game. Try to remember your husband loves *you*.

9. Men love a *vixen* in the bedroom!

   How true! How true! While husbands might have trouble creating a vixen environment, most men love their wives to be playful in the bedroom. This requires time, a little planning, and a husband and wife who are not drop-dead tired.

10. I do not believe in planned sex. However, planning can come in handy if you use the element of surprise for a vixen night. Farm the children off to a neighbor's house for a couple of hours, (promise to reciprocate!) light your candles, pull out that nightie, and put on your favorite CD. When your husband comes home after a long day at the office, it will surely flatter him and rejuvenate your spark!

11. Make your mind up to be sexy for your husband. Use all the gifts you were given, and have fun.
    Men, like women, want to be wanted. Our presentations may be different, but our end result needs are the same. We all want to be desired and loved.

BUT I WAS HERE FIRST! (YOUR HUSBAND)

With the birth of children, our focus and priorities change. Babies require so much attention and love that at the end of the day, moms feel loved out. The last thing we want as we fall into bed is another human being asking to be held. "For God's sakes, wrap a blanket around you. I'm going to bed!" Nasty feeling but honest. Moms give and give, and sometimes it feels like there's nothing left for our husbands.

But our husbands *are* important. The relationship we have with our partners is the greatest gift we give to our children. So, as wiped out as parents are, staying connected is a must.

These are some loving and fun ways to stay connected with your hubby for a lasting relationship.

FIND THE ULTIMATE BABYSITTER.

The ultimate babysitter is the backbone of all sane families. I know we want to be all to our families, but let's face it: moms need a break once in awhile, and dads need their wives to themselves once in awhile.

Finding a good babysitter may be a difficult task for some families. If you are unable to find one by word of mouth through friends or relatives, I suggest interviewing ladies that work in your local daycare programs and church daycares. Most come with references for you to follow up with to make you feel more comfortable.

If you have never left your angels alone with a sitter before, start slowly. Invite her over for coffee and introduce her to your children. Let the children see that you are confident and friendly toward the babysitter. This makes the first transition alone with her a little easier for the children and you.

You may want to go out for coffee with your husband the first time. Come back after one hour and see how everyone behaved. If things went well, then you are ready for a movie!

Finding someone that your children have fun with and that you feel confident in is the first step in having alone time with your husband. You can concentrate on each other without worrying the whole time if the children are all right.

DATE NIGHT!

Yippie! Once you have the children taken care of, it's time to plan your date night! Some couples make this such a priority that it's a set night out once a month. The first Saturday night of each month is designated as date night. This is an excellent suggestion if your work/children's activities schedules permit.

Otherwise you may have to look at your month ahead on a calendar, book the best night, and call the babysitter! However you work your date night, make it a priority just as you would getting your hair cut or your teeth cleaned.

Finding something interesting to do together can be great fun. You can use the Internet to look up concerts that are coming (you don't want to miss the Don Henley again, do you?), musicals, movie premiers, Christmas orchestras, football games, golf tournaments, or tennis matches. If financial constraints are an issue, pack a picnic and go hiking, ride bikes, walk around the mall, and treat yourselves to an ice cream. Take a walk though the city park. Or just sitting, sipping some really good hot coffee at one of your local coffee houses in their comfy chairs, uninterrupted and quiet, is wonderful!

It's not *what you do* that's important; it's *who you're with* that is the main event on date night. Spending a couple of hours getting reacquainted with one another, laughing and talking about your lives, uninterrupted.

Both of you are equally important in the family. Making date night a priority for yours is showing the same dedication toward your marriage that you have toward being good parents.

SECOND HONEYMOON!

If you could've looked into a crystal ball on your honeymoon and gotten a glimpse of the future, I'll bet you would've enjoyed that hotel room a little more, am I right? Clean sheets, room service, quiet, no Spongebob Squarepants, mints on your pillow...

Ask yourselves, when was the last trip we took *alone* together? If the answer is years, then it may be time for you to start the ball rolling.

There is nothing more exhilarating for a marriage than some time alone together. It doesn't mean you don't love your children; it only means you love each other *too*.

Our first trip alone together without the children was to Vail, Colorado. I left Christopher with Frank's mother and cried the whole week before I left. I was sure I was a bad mother for leaving a seven-month-old baby for four days. I contemplated canceling the trip numerous times right up to the very day we left.

When we landed in Vail, I took one look at the beautiful snow and mountains and immediately felt better. Still, I called my mother-in-law the first day five hundred times. We went to nice restaurants, walked in the snow… It was wonderful. For the first time in seven months, I actually saw my husband. What I mean is it was the first time I had taken the time to notice him. I had been so wrapped up in our new baby's needs that I hadn't taken the time to really see him.

I had forgotten how blue his eyes were or how beautiful his smile was when he laughed out loud. And this, ladies, is why you must make honeymoons and date nights a priority. Your husband needs you to remember how beautiful and precious they are too. Remind them how beautiful you are when you're smiling. Sparks don't just ignite on their own. They need a little elbow grease to get them started.

Of course, my mother-in-law was in big trouble from that point on because Christopher was happy as a clam when we returned. I realized that being apart could be a good thing for everyone, and now we drop our kids off with her all the time. Thank God for family!

Again, financial restraints may play a big part in getting away for many couples. Be creative! Look for hotel specials that offer free breakfast or a second night free. Even if it's just an overnight at a bed and breakfast down the street, plan it. Your family will be glad you did! (Well, maybe not your mother-in-law.)

Discovering again what you fell in love with in your partner is rejuvenating. Being in love makes us feel special, sexy, loved, and young again. Yes, we're tired from our workloads and middle-of-the-night feedings. But making marriages a priority is doable.

You can dress your children in clean clothes, nourish their bodies with healthy food, and teach them love and discipline. But the greatest of all gifts to any child is for a husband to love his wife and a wife to love her husband. At the end of your lives together, your legacy of love will live far longer than the memories of clothes you've washed and ironed.

Love your man.

You ... Even Lower on the Totem Pole? Caring for Yourself

The lights are blinding. You walk out on the stage and find your X put down with masking tape on the floor to remind you where you're supposed to stand for the best lighting. The audience is silent. You can feel their energy, waiting for you to begin. You purposely make them wait. It only adds to the drama. When you sing your first note, young and old alike cheer as though they are opening a gift they could have never fully anticipated.

Your grand entrance is interrupted with the squeaky voice of your seven-year-old asking if his friend Connor can come over to play *Transformers*. You quickly snap out of Live at Madison Square Gardens and remind him, "I am in the shower, young man, and I would appreciate a little privacy! We will talk about your friends coming over when I am dry and dressed!"

So much for your audience anticipation… And you were really about to belt one out too. As he leaves, you think, *How insensitive he is for cheating my fans out of the performance of a lifetime…* You finish shaving your legs, wondering the whole time, *What happened to me?* This thought is drowned out by your four-year-old crying that his older brother hit him in the privates.

Somewhere in between breastfeeding, making dinner, sewing Halloween costumes, making home-made Play-Doh, kissing boo boos, and ironing church clothes, a lot of mothers wonder silently, *What happened to* me?

I have to tell you it's a damn good question! All mothers love their children. We all want the best for our families. But there comes a time in most women's lives when they are looking at themselves in the mirror, wondering, *Where did I go?* It seems for some moms from the moment they say, "I do," to husbands and children, they say good-bye little by little to who they really are.

But what about the dreams and goals before this all-encompassing responsibility? What about your goals of running a marathon, being a writer, a singer, a scientist, a dancer, a doctor, studying dolphins, or being a teacher?

Let's face it: it's hard to be a stay-at-home mom eagerly pushing our husbands to fulfill their career challenges, ironing their shirts so that they look the part, hearing about their bonuses for a job well done while we get nothing concrete for our accomplishments.

I remember the first time I realized this was going to be a problem for me when my husband had gotten a new promotion. We were thrilled. It meant more money, more chance for moving up in the future, more stability. We already had two children with one more on the way, so this was positive news to be sure!

To celebrate I made a roast and mashed potatoes and a broccoli casserole that I'd never made before. When Frank got home, I must have asked him thirteen times, "Do you like my new broccoli casserole recipe?"

Finally he looked at me and said, "Honey, the casserole is wonderful, and please don't take this wrong, but you really need to get a life." Man, was he ever right.

When you have young children at home, a mother's positive feedback doesn't necessarily come in the form of a plaque or pay hike. It's probably more like your mother-in-law telling you, "You must really be a conscientious cook because Junior is making poopy at ten a.m., two p.m., and seven p.m. on the dot! Good job!"

Our husbands don't understand this need for feedback about our day. They think that being able to stay at home is gift enough. And they are right too. It is an extreme luxury and gift to be able to oversee the development of our children. After all, they miss the baby's first step, first words, the hugs all day long, and the first official run of patty-cake.

What is it that makes us feel we need more? I mean, is an official evaluation on company letterhead necessary to validate what we are doing? Unfortunately, some days it would be nice.

And what about working mothers? They get the company pat on the back, overtime pay, and even bonuses, yet still, even though there is not one wasted moment in their day, they yearn for their former selves at some point. They may be professionals climbing up the corporate ladder, negotiating deals, and scouring spread sheets everyday, but somewhere deep inside, at the end of the day when the last of the good night kisses have been dished out, she too is wondering, *What happened to* me*?*

Mothers are flesh and blood too. We give much and demand little, but the little we demand is so necessary to keep us afloat while we manage all the other lives of those around us. All of the people who *need* us. Our husbands, our children, our siblings, our elderly parents, grandparents… It's little wonder we even have time to shower each day. Denial of this doesn't do anyone any good.

Your happiness is important. Not only is it important to your well being, but it's mandatory to your family as well. The old saying rings true: *if Mama ain't happy, ain't nobody happy.*

So it follows that our next question is, what do you need to do to make you happy, fulfilled, and at peace with who you've become?

Notice I didn't include anyone else in the question. Your personal happiness is up to you. Each of us is only as happy as we make our minds up to be. It is not your husband's job to make you happy. (Although it is his responsibility not to make you *unhappy.)* Regardless of our marital unions, however, we are individuals on our own in the quest for personal-life satisfaction.

The following are but a few points to ponder when reevaluating your happiness level and how to get on the right road to a more satisfying life while taking care of your family.

STOP EXPECTING PEOPLE TO READ YOUR MIND (AKA MARTYR)

No one likes a martyr. They thrive on self-pity, and there can be no happiness found for someone who thrives on self-pity. You may need to accept the fact that your husband is *never* going to know that you would love to see an orchestra under the stars at an outdoor theatre. He is never going to get it that you would like to take ballet lessons again. It will not sink in to your husband's consciousness that you would love him to whisk you off to New York City, make reservations at Tavern on the Green for dinner, and hunt down tickets for a Broadway show for your birthday.

That doesn't mean he is a bad husband. Men and women just think differently. If you want a weekend getaway, go to a travel agency, pick up some concrete suggestions, and put them in his briefcase with a cute little note saying, "Just a few ideas for your wife's birthday, hint, hint!"

I know we'd *love* for them to do this automatically, and, granted, there are some men who would, but if you aren't married to one of them, no sense in standing around brooding about it. Nudge him along! Think of how much fun you would have together for a weekend away with no kids and how thrilled your husband would be to take the guesswork out of what to do for your birthday!

If a getaway trip is something important to you, help get the ball rolling to fulfill this fantasy! Being at home all day long with the children can be overwhelming for a lot of mothers. Don't wait for your husband, mother, friend to offer to take over for a few hours so that you can go to an afternoon movie you've been dying to see. Call them and ask them to baby sit. You might be surprised. Maybe they were waiting for the invitation to spend a little more personal time with the children, and both sides win.

By not expecting people to read your mind, you are opening yourself to a whole new world! Try not to allow yourself to fester in what could be. Communicate with the people around you who love you to make yourself happy.

DEFINE WHAT HAPPINESS MEANS TO YOU

This is harder to do than it may seem because our dreams may vary depending on the day we're having. For example:

Monday: Upon hearing your three-year-old tell you that you were a bad mommy because you refused to give in to another chocolate cookie, you may think that personal happiness lies somewhere between being a flight attendant only home on weekends and mountain climber, which keeps you away six months out of the year.

Tuesday: After watching your dog recycle his breakfast on your new rug, you contemplate an old desire to be a veterinarian where you could do more research on euthanasia.

Wednesday: By midweek you're watching the mountain of laundry grow and thinking to yourself how you might want to pay closer attention to your stock portfolio and investments. You studied investment banking in college, and, after all, a cleaning lady would be nice… So would a cook and a masseuse.

Thursday: After playgroup, some of the moms have mentioned several times how tasty your homemade chocolate-mint cookies are. They suggest marketing them on your own. You've always wanted to be in business for your-self and contemplate how you could actually do that and everything else you've got on your plate. It's an extremely exciting day just thinking about the realization of your own cookie business. You float on a silent high all day.

Friday: Oh, yes, that dinner party tonight. What to wear? What fits? As you go through your closet, you secretly reprimand yourself for eating the crust off of everyone's peanut butter and jelly sandwiches all week. You look in the mirror and determine that these thighs are *not* yours. As you pull out the same black dress you wore the last time you had dinner with the Thompsons, you vow to start Monday with a new and improved diet. You *will* lose twenty pounds. That's final. Plus, someone really needs to come in and claim these thighs and return yours.

Weekend: Your old inkling for science returns as you decide you want to donate your body to a sleep clinic. Poke me, prod me, but let me sleep.

All kidding aside, determining what makes you happy is crucial. No one can help you with this one. Try to be realistic; however, your dreams of running off to Holly-wood to be an actress may be over, but community theatre would be great!

Running a marathon is doable. You may have to get up and run at five a.m. before your husband leaves for work, but this dream is possible! You go, girl!

You may not be able to attain stardom by being the next Faith Hill, but you can sing in the church choir. If singing is what makes you happy, this is a wonderful way of meeting other women just like you, and most churches offer daycare while you practice!

If you've always wanted to be a dancer and open your own dance studio, start out small by putting an ad in your children's school newsletter. Push your living room furniture against the wall, plug in a small stereo, and teach four year olds beginner ballet. Their moms will love you for it!

The sky is the limit if you are realistic and patient. Remember, you don't have to go to the top to be happy. Learn to enjoy your dreams without necessarily becoming the best. Life is not about being the most successful painter since Van Gogh. Happiness comes from the *journey* toward being good at something.

GIRLFRIENDS!

Oh my, not enough can be said about girlfriends. No one on earth listens to me go on and on about my highs and lows quite like my girlfriends.

My best friend, Linda, and I talk at least twenty times a day. Our children get on the bus at eight a.m. every morning. This gives me five minutes to grab a cup of coffee. She calls me promptly at 8:05 a.m.

Girlfriends are for what my husband describes as mindless babble. Okay, I resent that. However true it may be, I love to babble. So shoot me.

We plan our schedules weeks in advance so that we can sneak out to the movies at lunchtime to see the latest chick flick. Anything with Brad Pitt, Richard Gere, or Hugh Jackman… We're there. I always feel sort of like

I'm playing hooky going to a movie during the day. It's wonderful.

I consider having girlfriends as a favor to Frank. I unselfishly spare him the details of the cute blouse I found on sale, the gossip about the school PTA president, and my menstrual cycle. Nothing makes a man cringe more than the mention of a period or mucus plug. My husband will volunteer to bathe the children while I call my sister to discuss a female problem.

Men don't need friends in the same capacity as women. Their phone conversations sound something like this:

Husband: Hey, Joe, wanna play golf on Saturday at three?
Joe: Sounds good.
Husband: Okay. See you then.
Joe: See ya.

Now, *our* conversations are a *tad* different. What guys can say in three seconds takes girlfriends about thirty minutes. Why? Because we are more colorful, visual creatures!

I want to know what you're wearing, get your opinion on what I'm wearing, ask you who is babysitting for you, tell you about my conversation with the pediatrician, mention that I have a huge pimple right between my eyes that I'm thinking may be a tumor, how I found the most awesome new facial moisturizer, and remind you to bring back the belt you borrowed.

Guys just don't need or desire any additional information. We women thrive on it. That's the big difference between men and women. The understanding of this psychological difference is the reason some couples make it and some don't. The marriages that do have a healthy respect for conversation fluff. I want it; my husband doesn't. Therefore, I must find other victims. Hence girl-friends. That's it in a nutshell. Amazing that some people pay thousands of dollars for therapy just to understand this simple concept. You're welcome.

If you don't have girlfriends in your life, giggly ones that like movies, funny children stories, shopping, bike riding, and gardening and are supportive of your cramps and in-law problems… get some. Be the instigator. Organize movie days, lunch dates, playgroups, museum visits, springtime nursery tours, and Bible studies.

Remember, don't wait for your doorbell to ring. The welcome wagon lady is long gone, sister. Make it happen for yourself. Martyrs don't make friends, but you can.

DIET AND EXERCISE

Blah, blah, blah. I hate to exercise even more than I hate dieting. I look at people running and think to myself, *What motivated her to wake up in the morning and say to herself, "I think I'll go outside in ninety-degree heat and pant and sweat until I can't catch my breath"?* This just looks so pain-ful to me. I would rather starve than run. I said *rather*. So I would just avoid both subjects altogether by not giving myself that choice. Therefore, I was free to do neither.

This is bad, bad, bad. Shame on me for thinking this way. I would look outside my window each morning and see all the mothers speed walking after the children got on the bus. I could've joined them, but then who would talk to Linda at 8:05 a.m?

This exercise avoidance worked like a charm until November 11th, 1997. My thirty-fifth birthday. It happened in one day. I woke up like every other morning, got undressed to get in the shower, and there they hung. My stomach, my butt, and the undersides of my arms. Overnight they sagged like a Christmas tree in January.

Of course the first thing I did was speed dial Linda. Perhaps there was an over-the-counter vitamin for this condition. She would know.

Unfortunately, she had only one remedy for my problem. I had to start exercising. You can only imagine my panic. Upon reinspection of my droopy hiney, I realized she was right.

The very next day, Linda and I joined a local gym and became aerobic stud-ette wanna bes. Aerobic stud-ettes are very serious about their work. They know all the moves, never take their eyes off themselves in the mirror, and rarely sweat. Their makeup and hair remain intact, as does their breathing.

The instructor reminded us not to get disillusioned by not keeping up, just to keep moving. I tried so hard. There were moments I was even able to do the grapevine and the step-up turn. Just as I was getting the hang of it, I realized that during the pelvic thrust, I had tinkled on myself. Hopefully they just thought I was sweating. A lot. So much for the joy of having big, healthy babies.

After about six weeks, I started to see a difference. The weight machines and aerobics began to lift my muscles back in place, and I surprised my boys with the lumps in my arms. "Don't mess with me if you want to live," I told them in my best Arnold Schwarzenegger voice.

The good news is that over the last couple of years, through watching the chips, potatoes, rice, and staying active, I have lost about fifteen pounds. I cannot describe how good I feel. I feel younger, sexier, and less grumpy about going to nice places because I am not so constantly threatened by the clothes in my closet not fitting.

The work-out phase, honestly, comes and goes. I would love to tell you that I work out for an hour each day. It's simply not true. But I do bicycle with my boys, take stairs instead of elevators, and swim. Could I do better? Yep. In fact, my goal is to get back on the tennis team when I finish this book. (Talk about professional disincentive!)

But whatever your physical activity level, find something to keep you moving and feeling young. Your diet and how you feel about yourself physically will dictate how you feel about yourself mentally.

Carve some time out of your day to walk the dog after dinner, jog before everyone gets up, or invest in a mini trampoline and jump during *Dancing with the Stars*.

Whoever said you only look as good as you feel was on to something. Just remember to wear a panty shield.

VOLUNTEERING

Volunteering can be a wonderful self-esteem booster for moms. When we give generously to others with our time and our talents, the feelings of accomplishment can be immeasurable.

Schools need our talents, churches need our time and hearts, soup kitchens need servers, women's shelters need a shoulder to cry on, hospitals need helping hands to play games with sick children, and the elderly need a young pair of eyes to read to them and bring them homemade jelly.

Besides caring for your own family, there is no other job that brings more fullness to your heart. Once a mother always a mother. The nurturing qualities that we possess should not be saved only for the people that we know.

You may find new gifts about yourself you didn't know you had! Volunteering is a great way to make a woman feel she is making a difference in the world. As if being a wife and mother weren't enough!

BLESSED ARE WE ...

Spirituality is the backbone of every family. Making time for prayer at the end of each day gives us a quiet time for the reflection of our gifts.

It's important to be grateful. By taking the time each day to remember that it is a blessing to be healthy, in love with your husband, surrounded by funny, loving children and afforded financial security, it gives us the perspective we need to gear up for each challenging new day.

Perspective is a powerful asset. To those parents who are staring out of a hospital room with a terminally ill child, the sound of children laughing is sacred. To the man in the unemployment line with three small children to feed, having a steady paycheck is not something he would take for granted.

So take the time each day to fully appreciate and give thanks for all that you are blessed with.

We are each blessed in a different way. Whatever your faith, I hope you will practice it openly with your family, not only to be the example but to exude the peace that is granted to those who have a relationship with their higher being.

Fill your spirit daily. What goes in must come out. Bless those around you with your peace, gratefulness, graciousness and faith, and you'll thrive on their rewards always.

DEPRESSION

Okay, there is a *huge* difference between being a little down once in a while and not being able to get out of bed in the morning. Call it hormones or the weather, but from time to time, we all feel blue. The key words are *from time to time*. If you are struggling on a daily basis to keep your head above water emotionally, you need to see a doctor.

Sometimes we get overwhelmed by the enormous task of being everything to everyone. These are the times we must step back and reevaluate what is important and what can wait to be done.

When I get overwhelmed by my life, I make a list of what I have to do. You would be surprised what you can delegate and even eliminate. You may have to reschedule some appointments to a time that is more convenient.

Sometimes it's okay to crawl back in bed after you get the kids off to school. Depression can occur from being overtired. If this is your situation, don't beat yourself up about it. Call in sick, cancel meetings or dentist appointments, and catch up on some rest.

However, a week of staying in bed, loss of appetite, or feelings of emptiness may indicate something other than fatigue is going on.

Contact a physician if you feel that you can't keep up with your daily responsibilities. With all of the new medications on the market today that are so effective and safe, it's such a shame that women suffer unnecessarily. Antidepressants no longer carry the social stigma they once had.

Some women may need some hormone therapy to help boost their mental well being. If you are concerned about how you feel, don't put off calling your physician.

Again, no one can do this for you. Make the call and feel better not only for yourself but for your family as well.

GIGGLE!

Laughter is indeed the best of all medicines. Looking at life with a sense of humor can make even spilled milk something to chuckle at… unless of course you just mopped the floor. This is *ungiggleable* stuff.

Serious people are no fun. If everything in one's life operates at a crisis state of emergency, then no one is enjoying themselves.

There are times where being un-fun is appropriate:

- Funerals
- Appointments for vein-reduction surgery
- Rotavirus

All other areas of your life are open game. If you can laugh at yourself, find humor in life's inconsistencies, then you are truly a giggle girl. If you can't find the humor in your life, surround yourself with people who can make you laugh. Rent funny movies, plan funny dinner parties, play Pictionary, read humorous books.

Practice makes perfect. Laughter is infectious. If your children are laughing, laugh with them. If they are whining, make a funny face or sing a silly song to get them to laugh.

In the greater scheme of things, the six-year-old neighbor Trey who just threw up in your five-day-old car is actually funny. Maybe not to your husband who opens the car door each night since you bought it to smell the new leather smell… But in time the odor will subside, and he too will be able to find the humor in little Trey's upset stomach. Well, probably not. (True story.)

I have found some of the most dramatic, chaotic episodes of all have made the best story-telling moments for later on down the road.

You may feel you're lowest on the totem pole, but you don't have to stay there. Where you fall on that pole is a choice we all make as mothers. If you choose to be a martyr with no life, no friends, no exercise, no diet to make you feel better physically, no faith spiritually, and no laughter (then you are boring… just kidding!), then you will indeed stay at the bottom.

Life has so much to offer mothers whether you work or stay at home with your children. Who said we can't have it all?

Reach out and make yourself happy. The top of the totem pole has a lovely view. The grass is greener, the sky is bluer, and spilled milk is actually comical.

Ladies, start climbing.

That's a Rap!

All mothers believe their children are special. (They are!) We all enjoy bragging about their accomplishments. However, very few of us are willing to tell... the *other* stories. The stories that happen behind closed doors or among strangers where there are no known witnesses. Fact is perfect children are merely a myth. There is no such thing.

My children are *close* to perfection. But 100 percent perfect? No way!

Christopher was only two months old when I found out I was pregnant with Josh. I was a tad overwhelmed to say the least.

When I went for the ultrasound to find out the sex of the baby, Frank of course went with me. I had mixed emotions. Part of me wanted a little girl with pigtails, and part of me loved the idea of having all boys.

The technician was very thorough and finally divulged without a shadow of a doubt that our new baby was going to be a boy. When she left the room, I looked into my husband's eyes and said, "Well, honey, looks like it's another boy!"

He said dryly, "You know they are going to pee on each other."

He had completely lost his mind, I concluded. I was horrified at the thought of my angels doing any such thing. Needless to say, it was a quiet evening at the Mathews' that night.

Fast forward a few years: I can't count the number of hand-written papers in my special drawer, written twenty-five times each, "I will not pee pee on Josh in the shower," "I will not pee pee on Sean in the pool," "I will not pee pee in Christopher's shoes." Frank was right. They did pee on each other. Still do sometimes. What is up with *that?*

Before closing out the book, I thought it might be helpful to dispel a couple very popular myths to help mothers let go of any unrealistic maternal quest in offspring perfection:

MYTH #1: YOUR BABY WILL STAY PRECIOUS

The truth is no mother can hold that darling bundle of pudgy flesh, heart pumping at the mere flash of a grin, and have any inkling that this angel, this gift from God will pee on his brother. But he will. And they will grow up and test your patience like you've never been tested before.

Those little smarty-mouth, ungrateful brats you see in the supermarket that you swear *your* children will *never* behave like that will more than likely be your precious baby one day. This is the truth about motherhood.

All children have temper tantrums at the most awkward moments, cry in church, break stuff, throw up on your silk blouse, and refuse to let grandma hold them at first. They will say embarrassing things like "Mom, why is that lady *sooooo* fat?!" while you're in line to check out with no where to run. They will bite other children at day-care and knock them down to get the toy they want to play with. They will grow into preteens and say things like *"You're not the boss of me, you know,* and *Who died and left you queen?"*

The trick is to never let them see you sweat. Stay controlled, set your rules firmly, take charge of the situation with minimum fuss, and laugh about it later when your husband comes home from work.

There is no getting around it. They will grow up, they will test you, and they will embarrass you. Be prepared for it.

MYTH #2: YOU'RE IN IT ALONE

I don't care what any other mother tells you. Her child misbehaves just as much as yours does. Nothing makes me more insane than to have a conversation with a mother who swears her children don't talk back, aim perfectly in the toilet, and don't fight with their siblings. Not true! If you run across a mom that says this, ask *her* to stick her tongue out. My bet says she's fibbing!

Each child comes with his own set of wonderful personality traits. Some children are creative, some athletic, some are musical, witty, or academic, just to name a few. But there isn't a mother out there who escapes. All children have a little extra something to keep us on our toes.

So try not to get caught up with the appearance of other families. You never know what battles are being fought behind closed doors. Perceptions are often quite deceiving.

Instead, concentrate on how you can handle your little one, and redirect him by giving a stable, loving home, firm guidance and discipline as tool to teach them acceptance and self-esteem. And, of course, laugh. A lot.

You're the CEO in charge. The next time you go to the sidewalk to call your little cherub home to eat supper and she announces to the neighborhood, "I don't have to listen to you!" Gently show her otherwise, knowing that all the moms listening at that moment have heard this before too.

At the end of every book, you should feel inspired. If you've just read a romance novel, you should feel lost and sensually charged. If you've just read an autobiography, you should feel compelled to live your life to its fullest with a determination to make a difference in our world.

After reading this book, I can only hope I have inspired you to enjoy your family. Hopefully you will walk away with some great tips on how to feed your family, be organized, fall back in love with your husband, and how to ride horseback on the potty… but mostly I hope I've inspired you to enjoy the ride of motherhood.

Laughter and love. They are all that matter in the scheme of things. At the end of your life, it's what people will most remember about you.

I mean, at your funeral, do you really want people saying, "Man, that Helen. She could fold some mean socks, couldn't she?" No, you don't.

Maybe our greatest accolades come when we are gone. Maybe that plaque, that bonus we yearn for, maybe it doesn't come in our lifetime. Maybe our good job is in the form of a legacy of happy family traditions that we start ourselves. A new breed of young men and women will go out into the world and make a difference because of the foundation filled with love and discipline we've created.

I don't know about you, but it's enough of an accolade for me.

Happy mothering and God bless!

References

Albers-Hill, Barbara. *Time-Out for Children.* New York: Avery Publishing, 1996.

Corwin, Donna G. *Time-Out Prescriptions.* Raleigh, North Carolina: Contemporary Books, 1996.

Dobson, James. *Dare to Discipline.* Carol Stream, IL: Tyndale House Publishing, 1977.

Lansky, Vicki. *Toilet Training.* New York, NY: Bantam Publishing, 1984.

Lansky, Vicki. *Toilet Training: A Practical Guide to Daytime and Nighttime Training.* Minnetonka, MN: Book Peddlers, 1984.

Pearce, John. *The Baby and Toddler Sleep Programme.* London. Random House, 1997.

Ramming, Cindy. *All Mother's Work.* New York, NY: Avon Books, 1996.

Siegel, Eleanor. *Keys to Disciplining Your Child.* Hauppauge, New York: Barrons Educational Series. Inc., 1993.

Varni, James W. . *Time-Out For Toddlers.* New York, NY: Berkley Publishing Group, 1991.

Additional Resources

PARENTING Guide to your Toddler by Paula
    Spencer
*Desperation Dinners! Home Cooked meals for Frantic
    Families in 20 minutes flat* by Beverly Mills
    and Alicia Ross
Betty Crocker's Slow-Cooking Recipes